Whittlin' Bill's FOLK CHARACTERS

Bill Higginbotham

Sterling Publishing Co., Inc.   New York

Dedicated to my dear wife, Frances, whose patience and encouragement helped immeasurably in the preparation of this book.

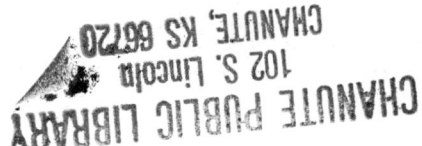

Edited by Vilma Liacouras Chantiles

Library of Congress Cataloging in Publication Data
Higginbotham, Bill.
   Whittlin' Bill's folk characters.

   Includes index.
   1. Higginbotham, Bill.   2. Wood-carving—Technique.
3. Caricature—Technique.   4. Wood-carved figurines—
United States.   I. Title.
NK9798.H53A4   1985   731.4'62   84-16349
ISBN 0-8069-7994-1 (pbk.)

Copyright © 1985 by Sterling Publishing Co., Inc.
Two Park Avenue, New York, N.Y. 10016
Distributed in Australia by Oak Tree Press Co., Ltd.
P.O. Box K514 Haymarket, Sydney 2000, N.S.W.
Distributed in the United Kingdom by Blandford Press
Link House, West Street, Poole, Dorset BH15 1LL, England
Distributed in Canada by Oak Tree Press Ltd.
℅ Canadian Manda Group, P.O. Box 920, Station U
Toronto, Ontario, Canada M8Z 5P9
*Manufactured in the United States of America
All rights reserved*

Contents

Preface 4
Acknowledgments 5
Woods for Carving 6
Whittling Knives 7
Carving Hands 10
Patterns 12
General Finishing 13

FOLK CHARACTERS & CARICATURES 15–49
Maria • Fritz, Igor & Ivan • Wan Qu Hung Hi • Franny & Freddy • Tootsigoots, Belle of the Ozarks • Jed • Ned, the Thinker • Mr. Bucks • Amazon Annie • Whiskers Willie • Farmer Fry • Flash, the Photographer • Fancy Dan • Casey, the Conductor • Whittlin' Bill

SPORTS GREATS 51–63
Fireball Feeney • Bowling Pin Benny • Cannonball Bates • Slingin' Shufflebottom, All-American

WESTERN HEROES & HEROINES 65–89
Stubby • Slim, Jim & Tim • Calamity Jean • Uncle Bub • Noodle Nose Nelson • Tom, the Toquerville Kid • Taco Juan & Hamburger Harry • Patch • Bucktooth Bill • Bucktooth Lil

GUNFIGHTERS OF THE WILD WEST 91–100
Big Ben • Fast Draw • Sure Draw • Shotgun Sam

MERRY MUSICIANS 101–125
Cactus Jack, Country Singer • Messrs. Sharps & Flats • G. Cleff, Choirmaster • Banjo Billy • Professor Higginsniffer • The Baby Grand

About the Author 126
Index 127

PREFACE

Creating human caricatures and characters from wood is, I believe, the most fascinating and challenging art form. Whittling not only prods the carver to use his or her imagination to its fullest capacity, but also develops a wide range of skills. Certainly, carving caricatures provides the ultimate in carving fun.

If you have completed the whittled figures which are included in my book *Whittling* (Sterling Publishing Co., Inc., 1983), you are ready to progress through this book. Since I demonstrated the basic techniques in *Whittling*, I will skip the preliminaries here. With a minimum of detailed instruction for most projects, I encourage you to take the plunge into carving human caricatures and characters. The projects are planned to progress for medium advanced to advanced whittlers.

In this book, I introduce the Dremel Moto-Tool as an auxiliary carving tool. With it you will be able to remove much unwanted wood with ease and speed. I only wish I had become acquainted with it many years ago.

Artist Fred G. Friese, who drew the many fine patterns for this book, sketched directly from the figures that I had created. This method produces accurate and realistic drawings.

After you have completed a project, try to vary the pattern—come up with your original caricature. For example, exaggerate certain facial features such as the ears, nose and mouth. In addition, you may want to modify the size of the hands and shoes. Since caricaturing involves the art of distortion, do not be afraid to experiment. I would like to share an anecdote with you from my teaching experiences (I began teaching high school arts and crafts in 1956).

In 1972, I was teaching an evening class for the city of Camarillo, California. One of my students, a well-trained artist, said, "Bill, I envy your carefree approach to wood carving. You don't seem to care whether your figures are in proportion or not. You just let yourself go and have fun. I cannot do that. I am bound by tradition and training received in the various art schools to strictly adhere to set standards governing proportioning." My student was right! Since I have had no formal art training, I have no inhibitions when I distort and exaggerate my creations.

I am quite certain that when you begin re-creating my whittled figures, you will become more skilled and confident. Soon, you will invent your own attractive originals and share my deep satisfaction that only comes from creating one of a kind.

Happy Carving!
Whittlin' Bill
St. George, Utah

Acknowledgments

I offer my sincere thanks to the following people and companies for their contributions and valuable assistance in the preparation of this book: Fred G. Friese, who drew all of the excellent patterns except those noted in some captions; Herbert Molyneux, who produced the many fine photographs; Dremel Division of Emerson Electric Co., which furnished one of its handy Moto-Tools and D-Vise; and Buck Knives, Inc., for providing me with a quality pocketknife.

I also thank Meyer Piet, who gave me two excellent patterns of gunfighters in 1972. I modified these patterns to produce several caricatures of gunfighters included in this book. My appreciation also goes to Van Smith who provided all the handcrafted knives except the bottom one in Illus. 1, which is the work of Herb Dunkle.

Woods for Carving

Aspen: Sometimes called quaking aspen, it is found in stands (clusters) in the higher elevations throughout the western United States. It is soft, resin-free and relatively free of grain. The heartwood varies in shades from white to tan. If you live where aspen is plentiful, try it.

Basswood (linden): I prefer this wood because of its close grain, even texture and pleasing color. For carving human caricatures and characters, basswood is unsurpassed. It is ordinarily free of knots, has no pitch or resin and does not split under the pressure of a knife or chisel, and lends itself to the delicate details of the face or hands. I select basswood that is slightly golden in color rather than white.

Jelutong: A very soft wood that is milled from latex-producing trees imported from Malaysian rubber plantations. Jelutong is easy to carve but not readily available. It is also becoming quite expensive.

Sugar pine: Another soft wood. I like the feel of sugar pine under my knife. The sugar spots in the wood enhance its warm, pleasing appearance. Select carefully. Some sugar pine is grainy and difficult to carve.

White pine: I like to whittle white pine because of its fine, even texture. It is soft with a smooth grain and an appealing color.

Miscellaneous woods: Willow, cottonwood, avocado and poplar are in this category. Some carvers prefer them to the above woods. I have experimented with all of these woods. I prefer basswood, white pine, sugar pine and aspen for human figure carving, however. The only exception is avocado which I often use for faces and hands. It carves like basswood and has a color similar to flesh tones.

WHITTLING KNIVES

Knives for whittling come in all styles and shapes. Some whittlers prefer large knives and others small knives. I knew a well-known whittler who used a large, Swedish sloyd knife to fashion the most interesting caricatures. Another famous carver used a variety of small, surgeon's scalpels to do everything but the initial roughing out.

I prefer to use a variety of differently shaped knives (Illus. 1). When I travel or accompany my wife on a shopping trip, I carry one of these quality pocketknives and whittle while my wife shops.

I use the knife instead of the gouge and the chisel because an expert carver recommended it in 1956. From the very beginning it seemed natural to remove wood with a knife. And it is convenient—I don't need to use a bench or a vise. I can whittle wherever I happen to be. Illus. 2 provides patterns to help you design a suitable whittling knife.

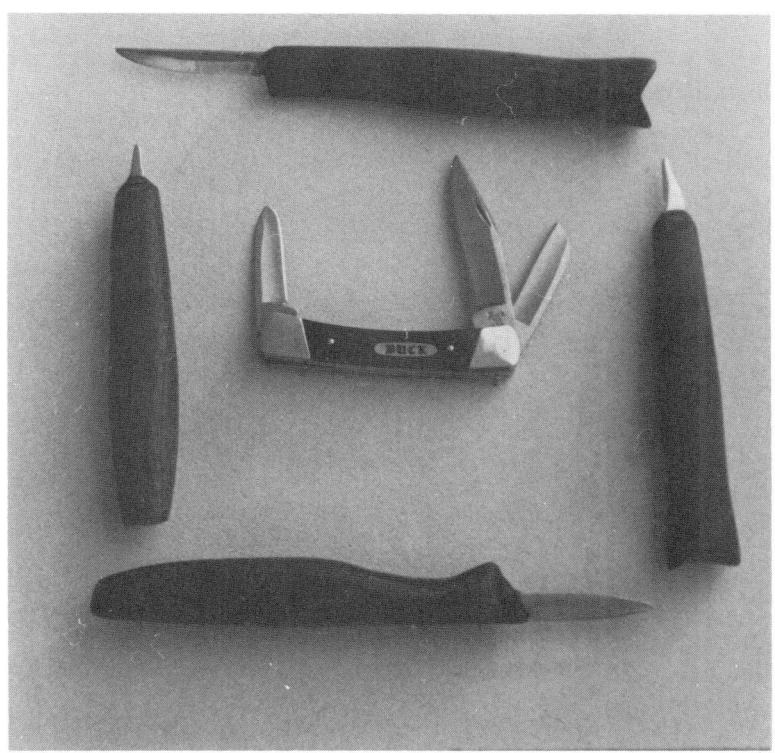

Illus. 1 Useful whittling knives. The pocket knife is furnished by Buck Knives, Inc.

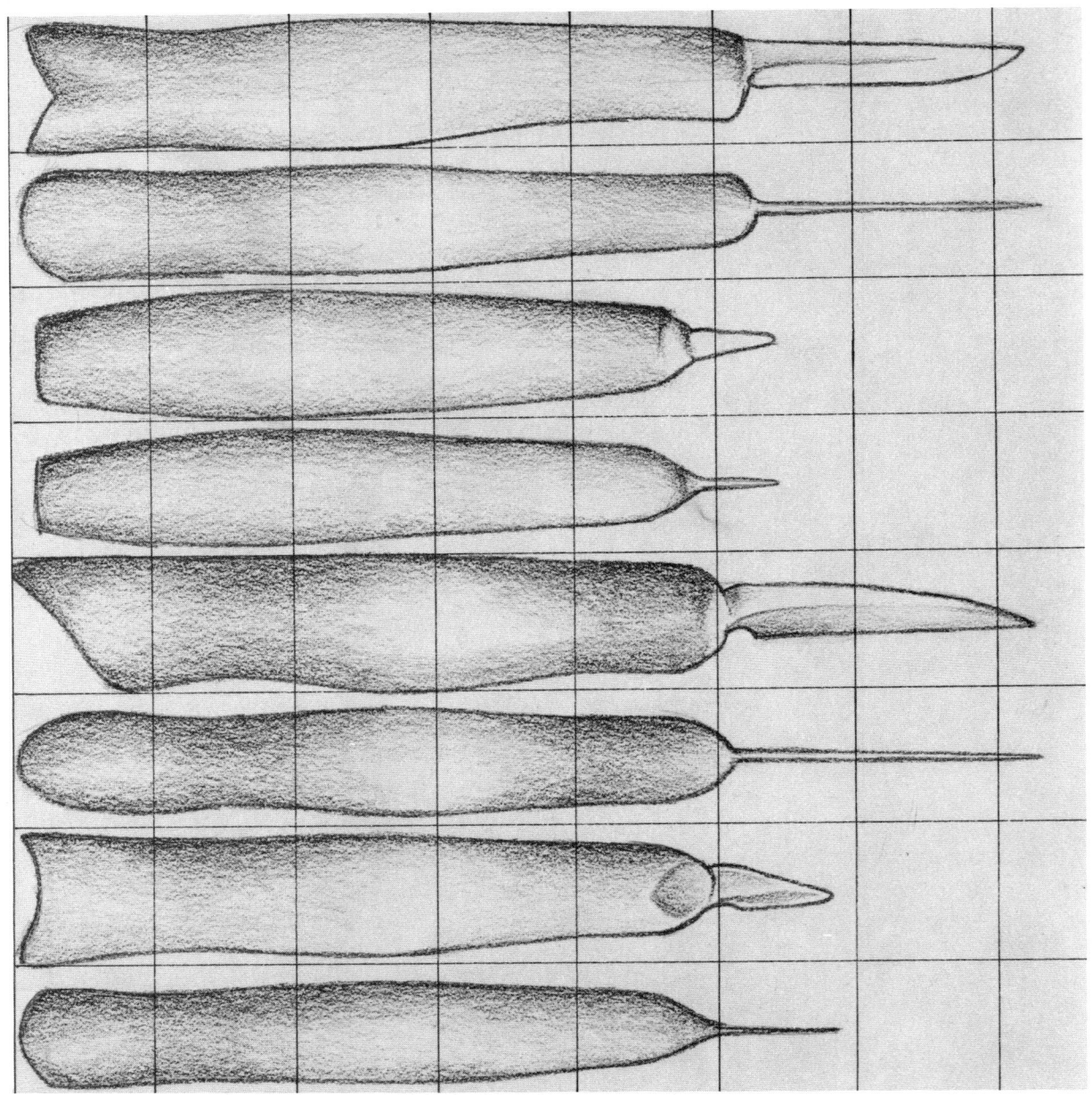

Illus. 2   An assortment of knife patterns. Drawing by Helen Caraveo.

SHARPENING KNIVES

It is good practice to keep your knife razor-sharp. A sharp blade is safer than a dull one and removes unwanted wood with less pressure and effort.

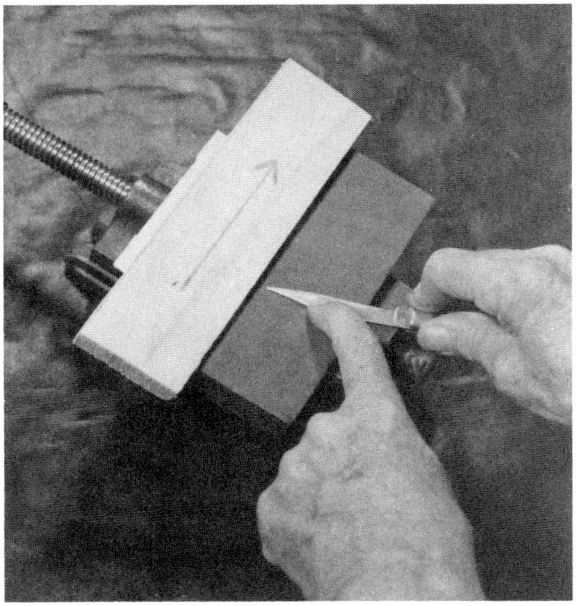

Illus. 3 Honing a knife on an oilstone. Apply pressure with your forefinger if the knife is ground flat.

Illus. 4 Stropping the knife on a leather strop.

Illus. 3 demonstrates a practical method for honing your knife on an oilstone. If your knife blade is ground flat, press it against the stone with your forefinger. First apply a generous amount of thin oil to the surface of the stone. This lubricant will wash away the fine grains of steel that accumulate from the grinding action as you move the blade back and forth across the stone.

If the blade has a bevelled edge, elevate it about 10 degrees. You can also use a circular motion to produce a consistent edge. First make several rotations in a clockwise direction. Count them. Then turn the blade over and repeat the same number of smooth circular rotations in a counterclockwise direction. Repeat these actions until you achieve a smooth, sharp edge.

To remove any burrs or wire edge, strop your knife on a leather as shown in Illus. 4. A strop is easily made by gluing strips of leather on a shaped board like the one shown in the illustration, 13¾ inches (34.9 cm) long. Apply a small amount of machine oil to the leather surface. Next sprinkle some fine Carborundum abrasive dust onto the oil. Strop the dust into leather with your knife. Impregnate the reverse side of the strop with jewellers' rouge. Again, use oil to help distribute the rouge. A few back-and-forth strops first on the Carborundum abrasive dust side and then the jewellers' rouge surface will keep your knife sharply polished. Do not overdo this procedure. Too much stropping will round off the edge.

Carborundum abrasive dust and jewellers' rouge may be purchased from lapidary or craft supply shops. You will find more detailed instructions on how to make strops in my book, *Whittling*.

CARVING HANDS

Carving the hands when attached to the figure can be difficult and troublesome. If you whittle the hands separately, you will encounter fewer problems. Should you make a mistake in shaping a hand, just discard it and start another.

It is easy to carve a hand if you follow my eight-stage carving sequence (Illus. 5 to 7). After blocking out as shown in Illus. 5, rough out the thumb. Then turn the hand over and deepen the palm. I use my Dremel Moto-Tool to rout out the inside of the palm (Illus. 6). Follow the three stages used to finish a grasping hand, the most common hand position shown in this book.

At first, it may seem difficult to successfully whittle a hand, but as you repeatedly carve this interesting appendage, it becomes much easier and more fun to do.

Remember to glue and insert the hand into the wrist hole only *after* you have finished painting or staining the caricature's sleeve.

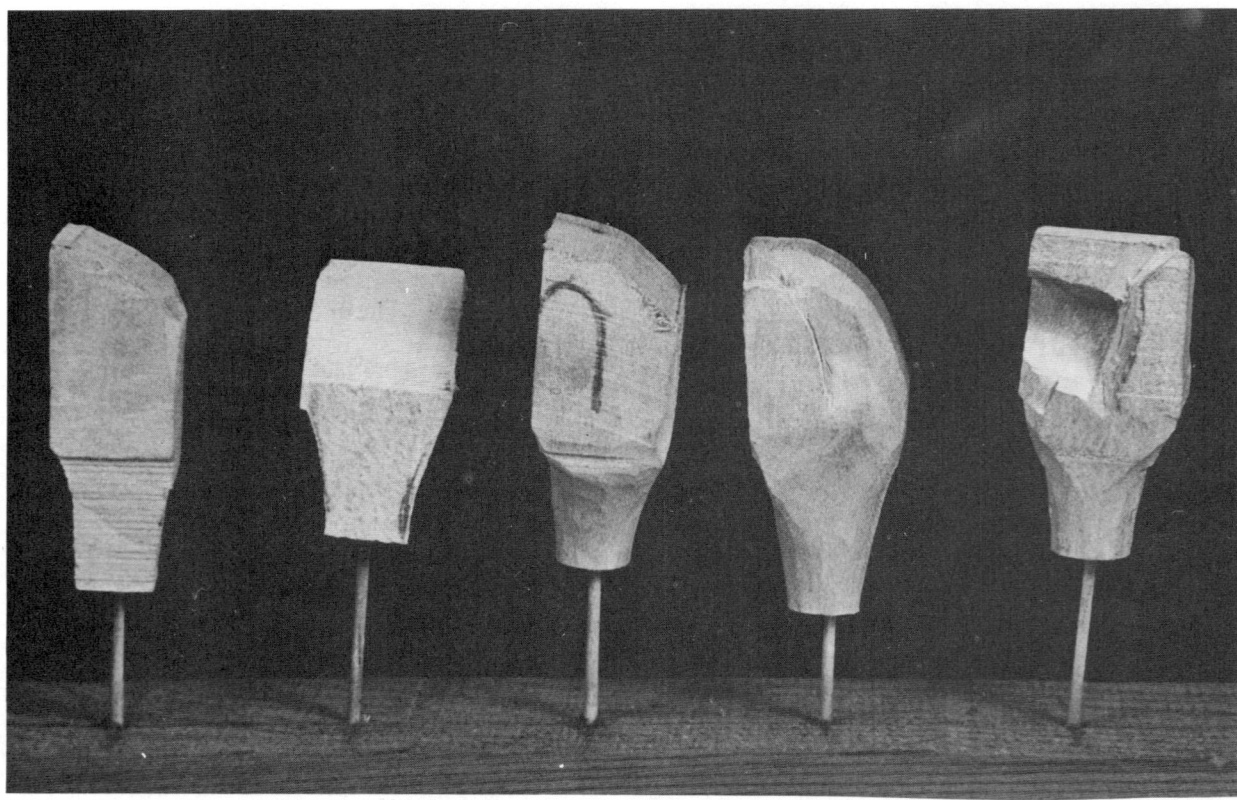

Illus. 5   The first five steps for carving a hand.

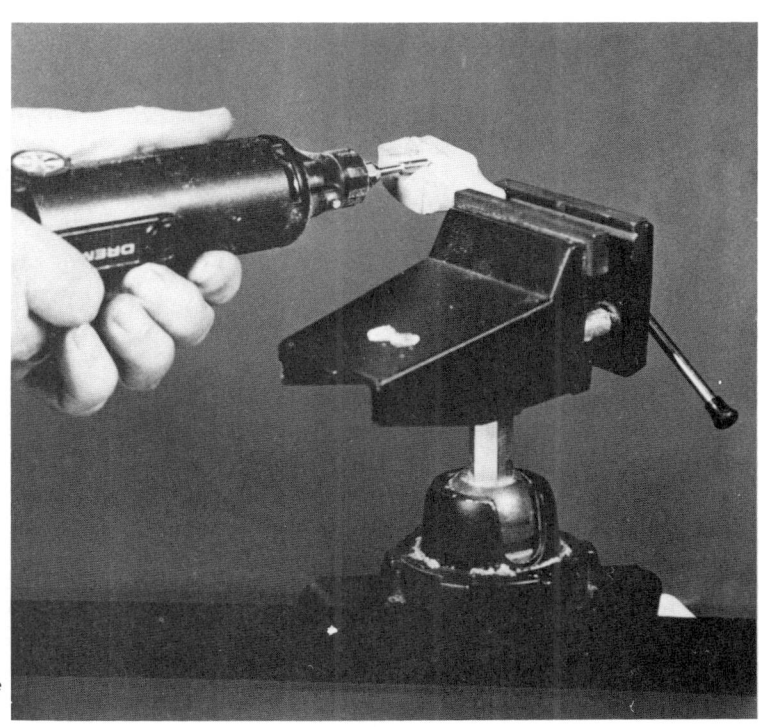

Illus. 6 (right)   Routing out the inside of the palm.

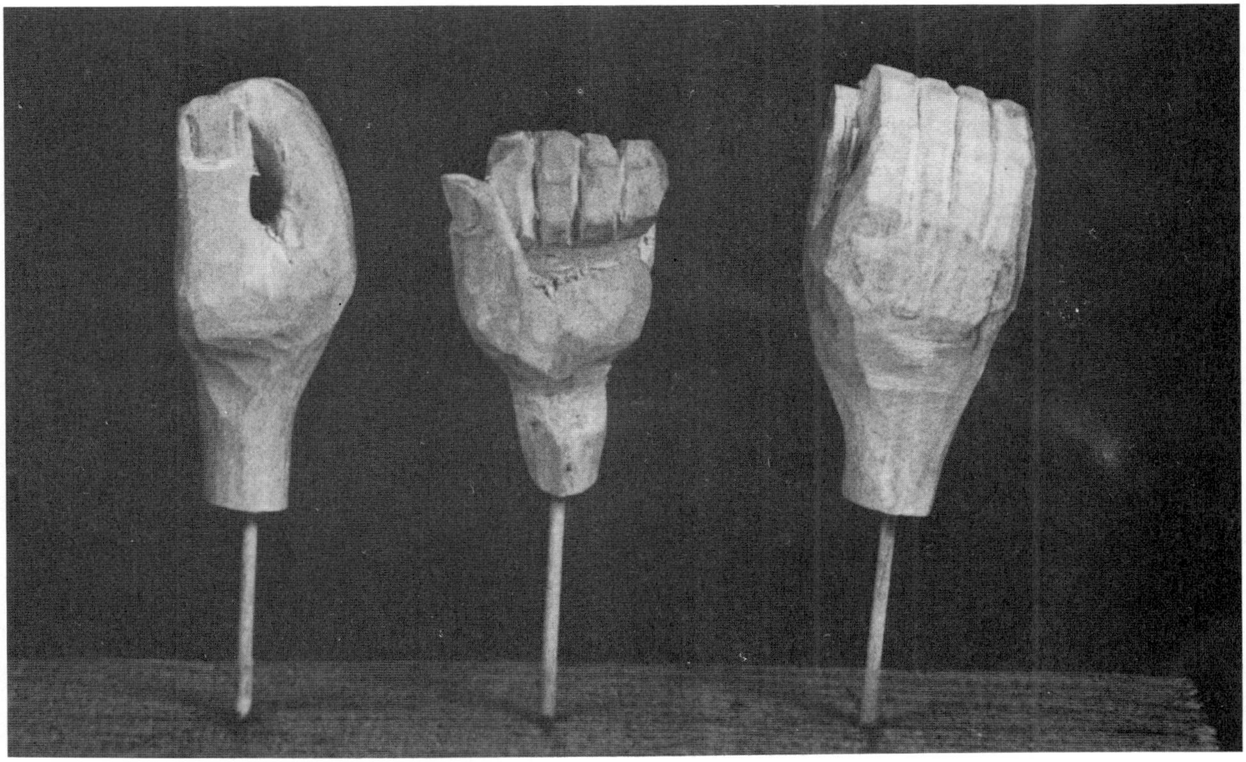

Illus. 7   The carved hand in the three finishing stages.

PATTERNS

The patterns in this book were drawn from the whittled figures to make them realistic and as close to the actual size as possible. If you prefer making the figures larger or smaller, refer to the instructions below.

To trace the pattern to your wood, place tracing paper over the pattern. With a soft pencil, outline the design with all the details. Hold the paper to avoid distortion, or better, mark the corners of the book page on the tracing paper before beginning. To draw the opposite side of the figure, turn the tracing over and outline all the marks. Using carbon paper, transfer the pattern to your wood (see markings on Fireball Feeney, Illus. 53).

To enlarge or reduce a pattern easily: make a simple grid or checkerboard as shown in Illus. 8. Use an easy grid, such as ¼ inch (0.6 cm), to mark off your original design on the tracing paper. If you want to enlarge this four times, on another piece of paper make a 1-inch (2.5-cm) grid using the same number of squares. (I usually number the squares on the small grid and number the squares on the larger grid before beginning the design transfer to simplify the task, and it works well for me.) Then, transfer the design square by square to the larger grid. This method is called "squaring-off," and is used by crafters in all kinds of crafts. If you prefer to reduce your design, simply reverse the procedure.

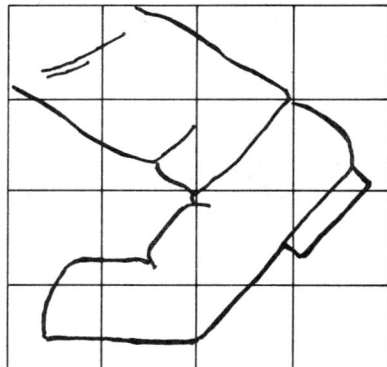
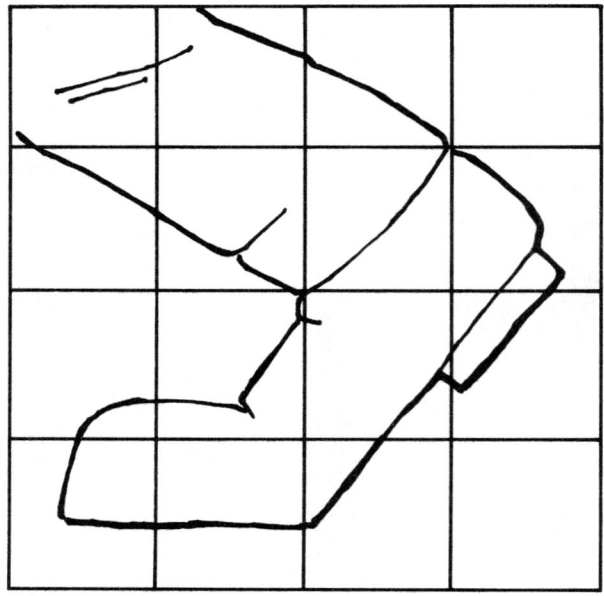

Illus. 8   The squaring-off method of enlarging and reducing a pattern is shown here. To enlarge the pattern, draw a larger grid with the same number of squares. It will not be difficult to transfer the design square by square, freehand, and maintain the original proportions.

General Finishing

Next to a natural wood finish, I prefer staining my carved figures. Too much paint spoils the natural qualities of a wood carving and detracts from the carved effect that is so attractive and desirable. A small amount of paint discreetly applied, however, will improve the appearance of your carving.

When finishing a caricature or character, I use the following process:

1. Remove all dirt and smudge marks by either carefully trimming the carving with a sharp knife or scrubbing with an old toothbrush saturated with soap. If you use the latter method, be sure to rinse well with clear water. Do not soak the wood.
2. After allowing the wood to dry thoroughly, spray the clean carving with a thin coat of clear varnish or lacquer. This will seal the wood so the stain will spread uniformly.
3. Before using oil stains, wax the areas to be stained with a thin coat of clear Trewax wax or Dorland's wax medium. (Trewax is available at hardware and paint dealers, and Dorland's wax in art supply shops.) Do not apply the wax to areas you plan to paint with water- or oil-based paints because the wax prevents paints from adhering to the wood.
4. When using stain, I prefer the various shades of walnut, mahogany red and Vandyke brown. Start with the lighter shades and work to the darker. Mix the oil-based stains with Danish oil, which dries fairly quickly to a durable finish. Paint thinner or turpentine may be substituted for Danish oil.
5. For a painted finish, use acrylics, latex paint or even artist's watercolors. Dry thoroughly.
6. When the stains are thoroughly dry, sand them with fine sandpaper to highlight the knife or chisel cuts. Apply light pressure on the sandpaper.

Do not be afraid to experiment with colors. Your color sense may surpass mine. Use contrasting shades as much as possible. Remember, paint and stain applied skilfully and judiciously may even improve a poorly carved figure. On the other hand, carelessly applied paint or stain can spoil a well-carved subject.

Illus. 9

Folk Characters & Caricatures

Illus. 10

Maria

I whittled Maria from an avocado limb. Since the branch was already rounded, it was rather easy to carve in the features. Perhaps you may be so lucky as to find a suitable branch and fashion Maria. If not, round off a piece of softwood 2 × 2½ × 9 inches (5.1 × 6.4 × 22.9 cm) and whittle this sweet little lady.

1. Before carving in the facial, hand and shawl details, dip her in water. This quick soaking slightly softens the wood, making it easier to whittle. Soaking also prevents chipping, which sometimes occurs when you work on small features. When you begin the finishing stages, keep a container of water handy for dipping.
2. Use a ½-inch (1.3-cm) gouge to plow the folds in Maria's skirt and shawl. Outline these furrows with V cuts made with a sharp knife or a tiny V gouge. Also cut tiny V lines in the lower edge of the shawl to simulate fringe.
3. Be careful when forming the exposed hand. If you make a mistake in carving it, however, merely remove it and fit and glue another hand blank in its place. Then whittle another hand.
4. Refer to Illus. 12 and note the deep cuts in Maria's face and the upper part of her shawl. Using an awl, perforate her head covering and the exposed part of her shirt to make many tiny holes. This will create a sweater or knitted effect.

FINISHING
1. Spray the entire figure with clear lacquer.
2. Apply clear artist's wax.
3. Stain her shawl and shoes dark walnut and her hair light reddish-mahogany. Leave the balance of the figure natural.

Illus. 11   Maria.

Illus. 12   Patterns for Maria.

Fritz, Igor & Ivan

Fritz, a German villager, makes a good companion for Maria (Illus. 11).

1. Using two pieces of wood, carve each leg with its shoe. Partially carve his body separately using another piece of wood. Then dowel and glue his legs to his partially carved body. After whittling his scarf, perforate it with an awl to produce a knitted appearance.
2. You will note in Illus. 14 that I pointed Fritz's shoes, thus departing from the pattern (Illus. 15). You may prefer to round them, as shown in the pattern.
3. Igor and Ivan (Illus. 13) are variations of Fritz. Whittle all three figures from the same pattern.

FINISHING

1. Clean and seal the carving (see directions under General Finishing, page 13).
2. Stain the head covering and coat medium walnut; stain the shoes and moustache Vandyke brown and the scarf mahogany red with a white fringe.
3. After the stain thoroughly dries, sand it slightly to expose the knife cuts.

Illus. 13   Fritz and his friends.

Illus. 14   Fritz.

Illus. 15 Patterns for Fritz.

Illus. 16   Ivan and Igor.

Wan Qu Hung Hi

I was in a rather zany mood when I started carving Wan Qu. My original concept for this figure was quite different. As I continued to whittle I became sidetracked into doing this rather humorous oriental caricature. This is not the only time that I have had this experience.

1. Carve Wan Qu's head separately from his body. I have done this with most of the figures in this book. I carve the head separately whenever it is feasible. There are advantages in carving the head separately. It enables you to use semihard woods for the heads and softwoods for the bodies. The semihard woods are more suitable for carving small, detailed facial features. The softwoods used for the bodies are easier to whittle. Wan Qu's head is basswood and his body is aspen.

2. Since the head is separate, it may be turned in any desired direction. I seldom glue the head to the body, but rather attach it loosely with a ¼-inch (.6-cm) dowel.

FINISHING

1. Clean and seal the wood (see directions under General Finishing, page 13).

2. Paint his hair, coat buttons and shoes black. Paint his hair ribbon bright red and his teeth off-white. His body was left unpainted—natural wood color.

Illus. 17   Wan Qu Hung Hi.

Illus. 18 Patterns for Wan Qu Hung Hi.

Franny & Freddy

Togetherness is an apt expression to describe this happy couple.

1. In order to simplify the carving of Franny and Freddy, block them out with a band saw. Then carefully part them down the middle dividing line with the band saw (see Illus. 21).
2. As you partially carve both figures, leave untouched the surfaces to be joined later.
3. To join them, apply wood glue to the uncarved surfaces and press the two figures tightly together with your hands until the glue sets. To make certain that the dividing seam will not be noticeable, place the glued figures in a vise and apply additional pressure. Wait until the glue dries thoroughly.
4. Whittle the figures to their final forms.

FINISHING

1. Clean, seal and wax the parts to be stained (see directions under General Finishing, page 13).
2. Apply the following colors: stain Franny's dress mahogany red, shoes and hair medium walnut and paint her socks, collar and teeth off-white. Stain Freddy's coat and hair dark walnut, his shoes Vandyke brown and paint his socks bright red. Paint his coat buttons black, his teeth off-white and leave his trousers the natural wood color.

Illus. 19   The inseparable Franny and Freddy.

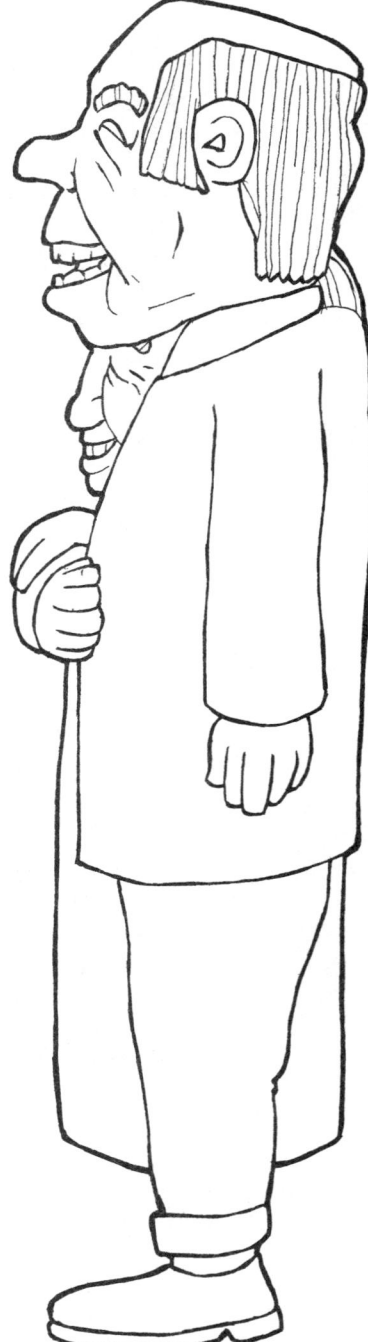

Illus. 20 Patterns for Franny and Freddy.

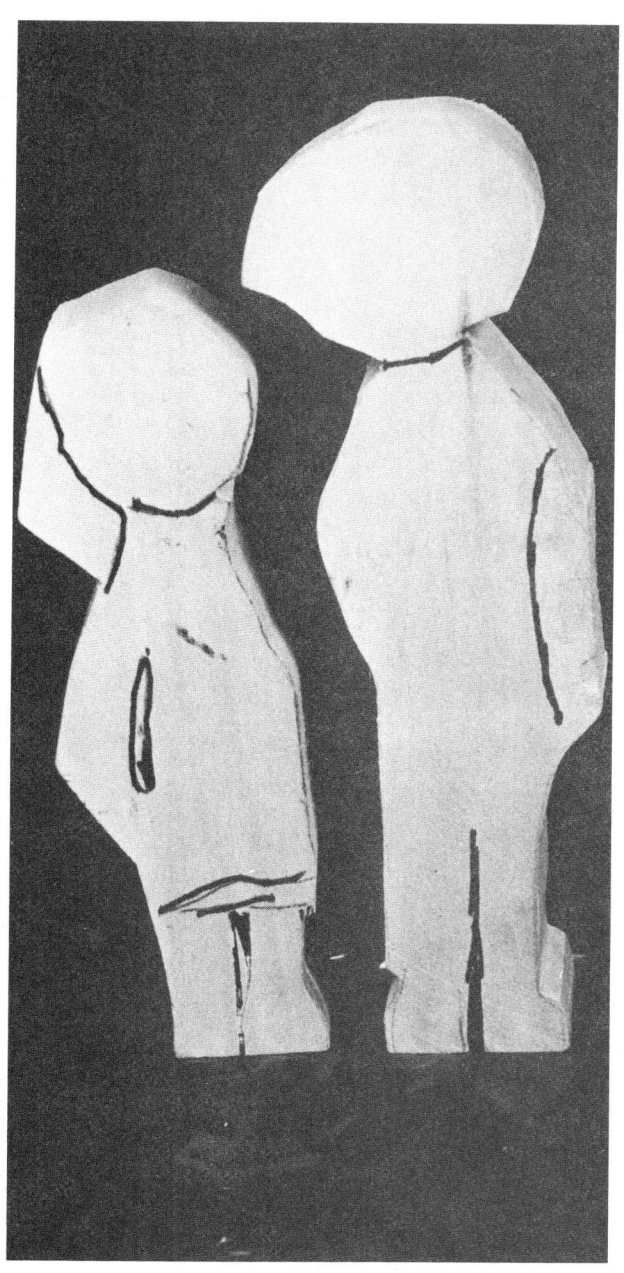 

Illus. 21   Franny and Freddy blocked out and separated.

Illus. 22   Franny and Freddy from the back.

Tootsigoots, Belle of the Ozarks

This rather striking little lady should provide you with several hours of interesting work. Her oversized shoes prevent her from falling on her nose.

In order to use some scrap wood, I decided to carve her in three sections—head, body and shoes with legs. After carving each part separately, I drilled two holes into the underside of her dress to accommodate the legs and a neck hole for her head.

FINISHING
1. Clean and seal the figure (see directions under General Finishing, page 13).
2. Stain her hair dark walnut, apron light mahogany red and her shoes Vandyke brown. Paint her dress off-white, socks bright red and her belt and buttons black.
3. When the paint and stain dries, glue the legs into the drilled holes.
4. Fit her head loosely into the neck hole.

Illus. 23   Tootsigoots stands on oversized shoes.

Illus. 24   Tootsigoots showing her new hairdo.

Illus. 25   Patterns for Tootsigoots.

Jed

Jed is another character that I whittled from three separate pieces of wood.

1. Saw out his body and the barrel portion from a single piece of softwood.
2. Part the barrel section from his body with a band saw.
3. Carve all details of his body and the barrel.
4. Attach them loosely with a ¼-inch (.6-cm) dowel.

If you prefer, you can whittle Jed's head and his hat separately. Refer to the project Stubby for detailed instructions describing this process.

FINISHING

1. Clean and seal (see directions under General Finishing, page 13).
2. Paint Jed's overalls with a thin coat of blue watercolor, his shirt off-white, his tie and handkerchief bright red. Stain his hair, hat and shoes Vandyke brown, the

Illus. 27 The front view of Jed.

barrel staves light walnut and the hoops dark walnut.

3. When the stains and paints dry, glue the barrel in place.
4. Lightly sand over the blue watercolor paint and the stains to complete the job.

Illus. 26 Jed relaxes on a barrel.

Illus. 28   Patterns for Jed.

Ned, the Thinker

Carving Ned is similar to the procedure used for fashioning Jed (Illus. 27). I also used the same basic pattern for both figures. The main differences between the two carvings are their clothing, heads, hats and the position of their hands.

If you have already completed Jed, you can easily whittle Ned. Carve Ned's cap and head out of one piece of semihard wood, however.

FINISHING

1. Clean and seal your carving (see directions under General Finishing, page 13).
2. Stain Ned's trousers light walnut and his cap, coat and shoes dark walnut.
3. Paint his shirt off-white and the stripes of his tie black and red.
4. Stain the barrel staves light walnut and the hoops dark walnut.

Illus. 29   Ned contemplating.

Illus. 30   A front view of Ned.

Illus. 31   Patterns for Ned.

Mr. Bucks

Years ago, I saw a photograph of a businessman gazing at a painting. The photo was taken from behind him, therefore only the back of the gazer was visible. I was curious to see what he looked like from the front, so I whittled him in the round. The result is Mr. Bucks (Illus. 32 and 33).

1. I carved his head and hands separately out of avocado wood and his body from aspen. Substitute any suitable wood you like.
2. Whittle his hat separately and fit it between the thumb and forefinger of his right hand (Illus. 32).
3. To take advantage of the lengthwise grain, carve his shoes separately and glue them to the ends of his legs.
4. Use the umbrella pattern in Illus. 34 for your convenience.

FINISHING

Paint his coat, trousers and hat light blue-grey and his shirt white. Paint his tie and handkerchief dark blue and the umbrella black.

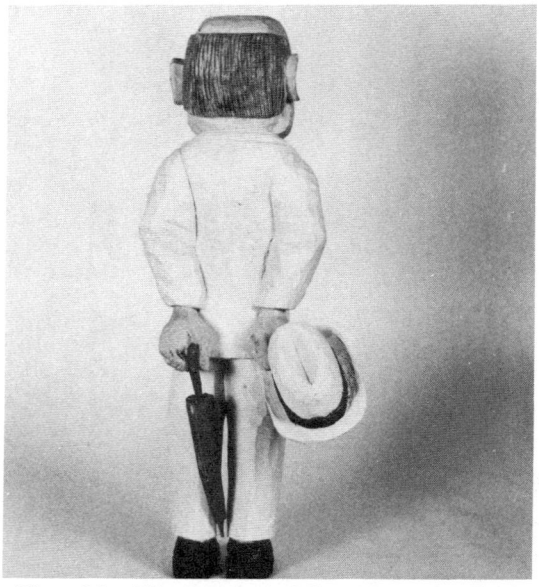

Illus. 32   Mr. Bucks holding his umbrella and hat.

Illus. 33   Mr. Bucks poses for a photo.

Illus. 34 Patterns for Mr. Bucks.

Amazon Annie

Annie may look tough but, on the contrary, she has a heart of pure gold. She would give you the shoes right off her feet, if she felt you needed them.

I whittled her unusual head from a piece of a distorted avocado branch. Having little to do one evening but watch a boring television movie, I fetched a piece of avocado limb from my odds-and-ends box and began shaping Annie's head and features. The experience of creating something unique from what seemed to be a hopeless piece of wood developed into a pleasant and a profitable two hours.

1. Using a piece of jelutong (or other softwood), whittle her handbag.
2. For the handle, shape a piece of hardwood.
3. After carving the bag and the handle to final form, drill a hole through her hand just large enough to accommodate the handle. In order to insert the handle through this hole, cut the handle into two sections. Then glue the handle ends into small holes drilled into the handbag. Leave Annie's hand loose around the handle so the bag can swing freely.
4. Whittle her shoes separately. Drill holes into her shoe tops. Then fit her sturdy legs into the holes.

FINISHING

Paint her shirt off-white, the buttons black and her socks yellow. Then stain her skirt mahogany red and her shoes and hair Vandyke brown. Leave her handbag natural.

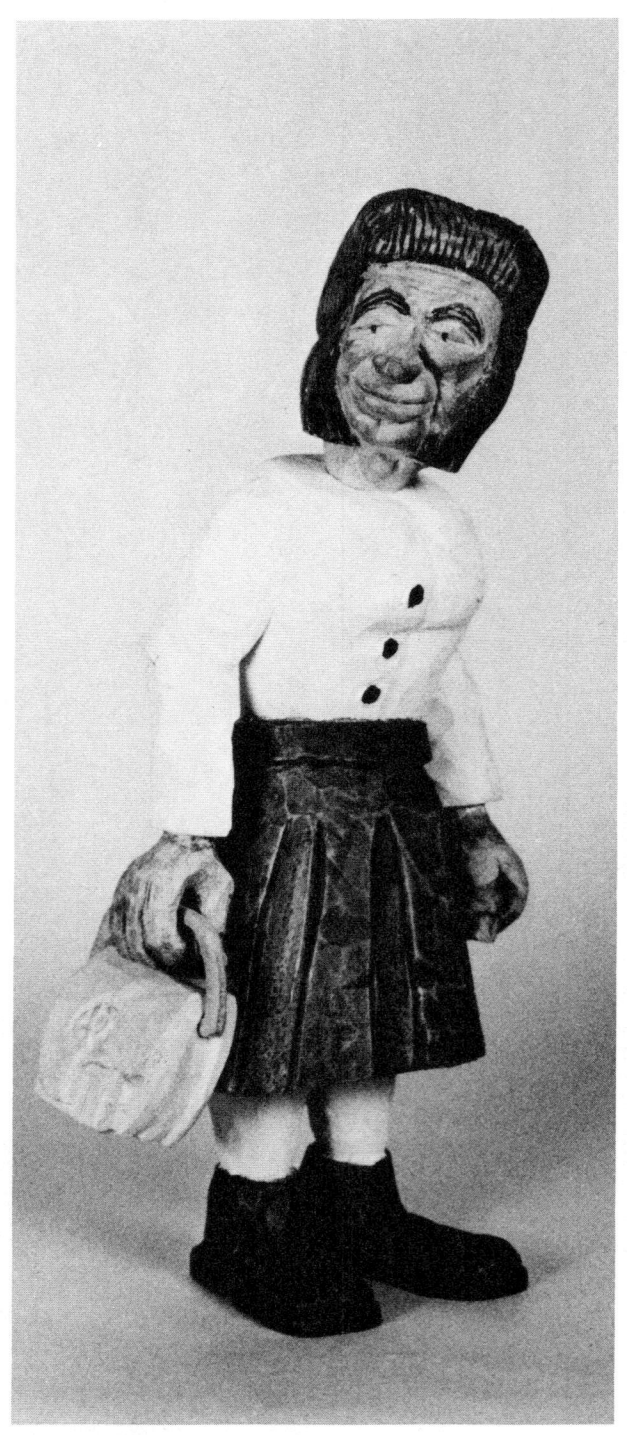

Illus. 35   Amazon Annie.

Illus. 36 Patterns for Amazon Annie.

Whiskers Willie

Willie's extra-long beard is an attention-getter. Also, his downswept moustache enhances his debonair appearance. Clutching his top hat and his cane, he is indeed ready to make a conquest.

1. Carve his body and his head out of one piece of avocado wood.
2. In order to make it easier, fashion his hat and left hand separately from his arm out of a single piece of avocado wood.
3. It is easy to whittle a cane and thrust it through a hole drilled in his right hand.

FINISHING

Stain his trousers light walnut, his whiskers, hair and coat dark walnut. Then paint his boots, hat and cane black. Leave his vest natural wood color.

Illus. 37 Whiskers Willie.

Illus. 38 A rear view of Willie.

Illus. 39 Patterns for Whiskers Willie.

Farmer Fry

This ambitious farmer, our first action figure, presents an interesting challenge. Farmers particularly enjoy him.
1. Whittle his hat and body from aspen.
2. Carve his head and hands from avocado or any semihard wood.
3. A short section of tree limb can serve for the milk pail. Use a 3-inch (7.6-cm)-long piece of stiff copper wire for the bail (arched handle).

FINISHING
Stain Fry's hat dark walnut, his hair medium walnut, and his boots Vandyke brown. Leave the remainder of the figure natural wood color.

Illus. 40   The farmer goes a-milking.

Illus. 41 Patterns for Farmer Fry.

Flash, the Photographer

Flash is a favorite among camera buffs. Since his head is hidden, he is not too difficult to carve.

1. Begin with the lower part of his body separately; this includes the section from the exposed part of his shirt down to and including his shoes. Use a 2-inch (5.1-cm)-thick piece of softwood for this part of the figure.
2. Cut out and shape the upper half from a piece of 3-inch (7.6-cm)-thick wood; this includes the upper torso, arms and the cape.
3. Cut out the camera and its support base separately from the cape section. Shape the camera and its base to completion.
4. Next, whittle the hands and their props.
5. Taper three 3/16-inch (4.76-mm) dowels for the camera tripod.
6. Glue the camera and its base to the front of the cape.
7. After the glue dries, drill three holes at the proper angles into the underside of the camera base for the dowel legs. Do not glue the lower torso to the upper yet.

FINISHING

1. Stain the trousers light walnut and the shoes Vandyke brown.
2. After masking the arms, vest, shirt and the lens sections, spray the exposed cape, camera and dowel supports with flat black paint.
3. When the paint dries, dowel and glue the upper and lower torsos together.
4. Next, paint the camera lens, arms and the exposed part of his shirt off-white. Decorate his arm garters black and red, leaving his vest natural wood color.
5. As soon as the paints and stains are thoroughly dry, lightly sand the black paint and the stained surfaces.
6. Dowel and glue the left shoe to a base carved to simulate a box (Illus. 42).
7. Glue the props into their respective hands and the hands into their sleeves.
8. Complete this project with several coats of clear wax applied to the base.

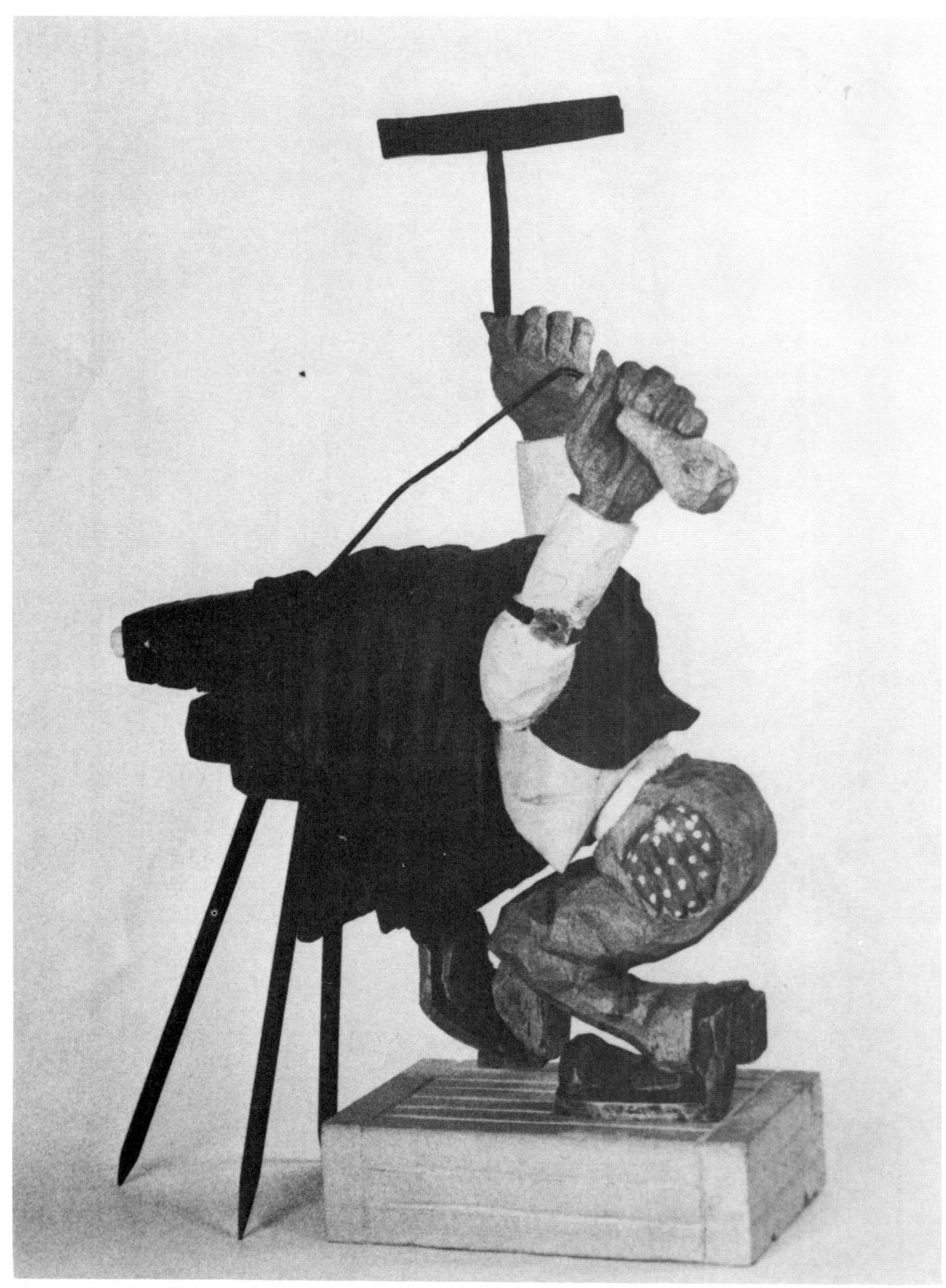

Illus. 42 Say "Cheese."

Illus. 43   Pattern of Flash (right side).

Illus. 44   Pattern of Flash (left side).

Fancy Dan

Fancy Dan, a ladies' delight, is all spruced up, ready to escort his date to the nearest ice-cream shop.

1. Carve his hat and head from two separate pieces of wood. Glue and press them together in a vise.
2. Fashion his flower from two pieces, the stem separate from the petal section.
3. To take advantage of running the grain along the length of the shoes, whittle them together with their ankles. Then insert the ankles into holes that you previously drilled into the ends of his legs.

If you wish to substitute a cup for the posy (as shown in Illus. 46), use the hand and cup pattern on Illus. 47.

FINISHING

Paint his shirt, socks and teeth off-white and his tie bright green. Paint his flower as follows: stem bright green, petals yellow and the seed bed brown and orange. Then, paint his hat, coat and shoes with flat black paint, leaving his trousers natural wood color.

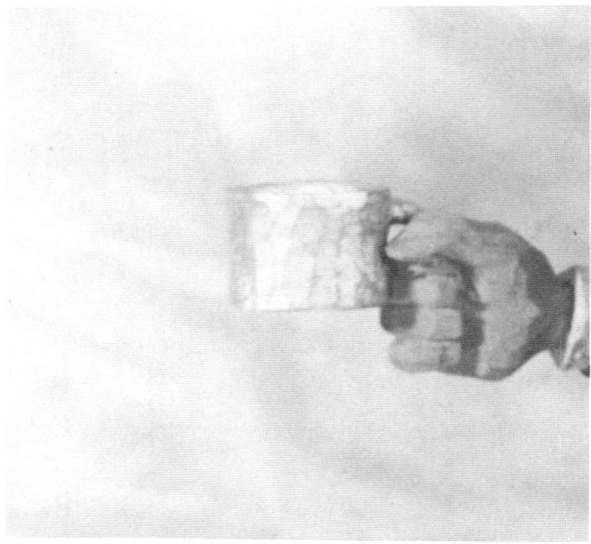

Illus. 45 "Brother, lend me a fiver."

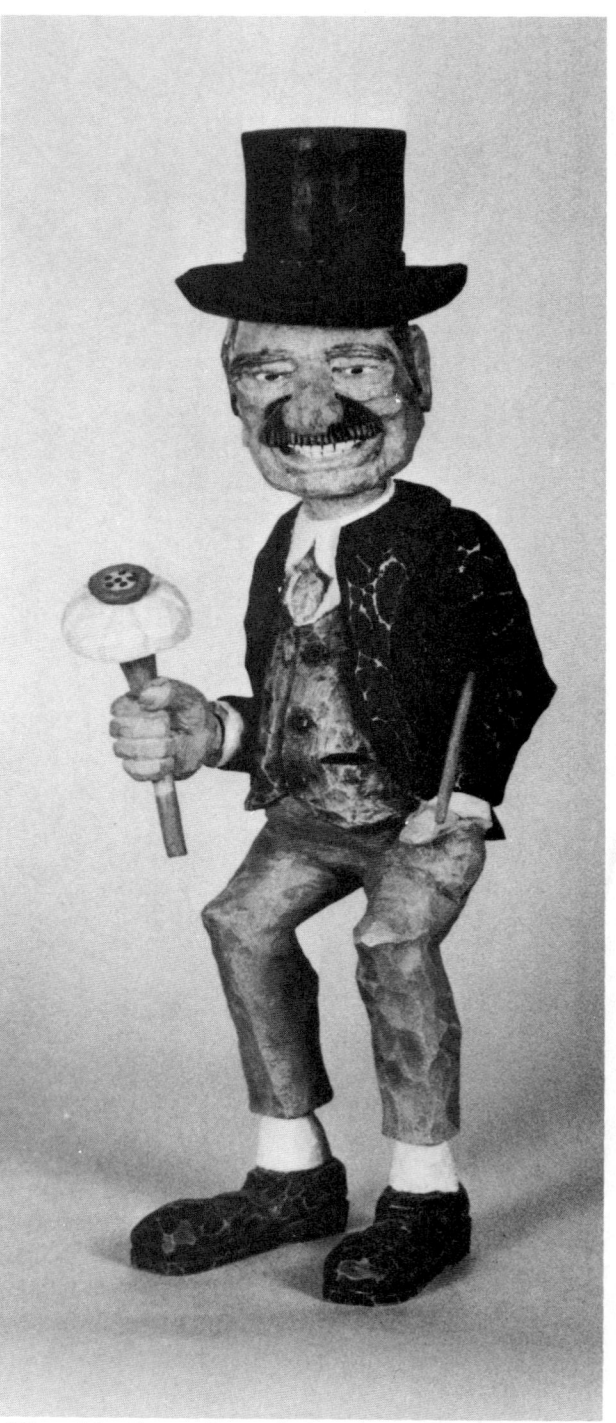

Illus. 46 Fancy Dan all dressed up for his date.

Illus. 47 Patterns for Fancy Dan.

Casey, the Conductor

To carve Casey, just follow the procedure similar to the one described in the project Fancy Dan (Illus. 46).

If you have difficulty carving the watch as part of the hand, from time to time hold a pocket watch in your hand as a model. For more assistance, refer frequently to the pattern (Illus. 49) and the photo (Illus. 48).

Whittle the lantern separately and suspend it loosely from his left hand with a carved wooden bail.

FINISHING
1. After masking all sections of Casey except his hat, coat and shoes, spray the unmasked parts with flat black paint.
2. Stain his vest mahogany red and his hair and moustache dark walnut. Then, paint his trousers light grey, his shirt off-white, and tie bright green. Paint the glass part of his lantern yellow and its cage black.

Illus. 48   "All aboard!"

Illus. 49 Patterns for Casey, the Conductor.

Whittlin' Bill

Some of my friends told me that this figure resembles me, the author of this book. It was not my intention to whittle a self-portrait. Therefore, any resemblance between this carving and myself is purely coincidental.

1. Cut Bill's lower torso and his stool seat from a single piece of wood and his upper half from another piece. For the lower half, use 2-inch (5.1-cm) stock and for the upper 3½-inch (8.9-cm) stock. Whittle his head, hands and their props separately. Carve his head from a 2-inch (5.1-cm)-thick wood.

2. Whittling his legs in the crossed position is not too difficult if you work on each leg alternately, carving for short intervals of time. It also helps to visualize the position of the legs if you can sit in front of a mirror while doing this part of the figure. The little log supporting his left leg is for balance and stability.

3. Whittle the stool legs separately and glue them into holes drilled into the underside of the seat. Suggestion: drill 1/16-inch (1.59-mm)-diameter holes for the stool leg cross supports before you start to whittle the legs.

FINISHING

Stain his trousers light walnut, his vest mahogany red, and shoes and hair dark walnut. Paint his shirt off-white and stripes of his tie black and green.

Illus. 50   Whittlin' Bill at work.

Illus. 51   Patterns for Whittlin' Bill.

Sports Greats

Illus. 52

Fireball Feeney

Fireball is shown in his classic pose before throwing his famous "smokeball." It is easier to carve Fireball Feeney if you use the wood- and time-saving method of multi-piece carving described below. Not only will you be able to use wood scraps, but you will be able to position the parts before gluing them in place. You also can arrange the pieces with the grain running lengthwise for greater strength.

1. Trace on paper all the body parts shown in Illus. 54 and transfer the tracings to various pieces of softwood. Use 2-inch (5.1-cm)-thick wood for the lower torso and 1¾-inch (4.4-cm)-thick wood for the upper. Cut the arms from 1-inch (2.5-cm)-thick wood and the head from 2-inch (5.1-cm)-thick, semihard carving wood. Since the left arm is a duplicate of the right, use the same pattern for both arms. Saw out the parts as shown in Illus. 55.
2. Dowel and glue the upper torso to the lower torso (Illus. 56). Press and hold these two sections in place until the glue dries. Next, drill a ¾-inch (1.9-cm)-diameter hole between the shoulders to receive the neck.
3. Rough-carve the assembled body to shape.
4. Drill holes in the ends of the arms to receive the wrists.
5. Whittle the arms and shoes to almost finished form. Then glue these sections to the body and the legs as shown in Illus. 57, 58 and 59. Drill holes into the ends of the arms for the hands. Illus. 60 shows the figure assembled. Now you are ready for the final shaping and carving the details.
6. Carve the head and cap. I used my Dremel Moto-Tool to remove excess wood under the brim of the cap.
7. Use the hand patterns (Illus. 54) for aid in whittling those sections. Glue the finished hands into the holes you drilled in step 5.
8. Finish carving the body (Illus. 60).

FINISHING
1. Stain the cap, shirt and socks mahogany red. Stain the baseball glove and shoes medium walnut and his hair, moustache and shoe soles Vandyke brown. Then, paint the belt black and the baseball white.
2. After the stains are thoroughly dry, sand them lightly to expose and emphasize the knife cuts.

Illus. 53   Fireball Feeney at the peak of his windup.

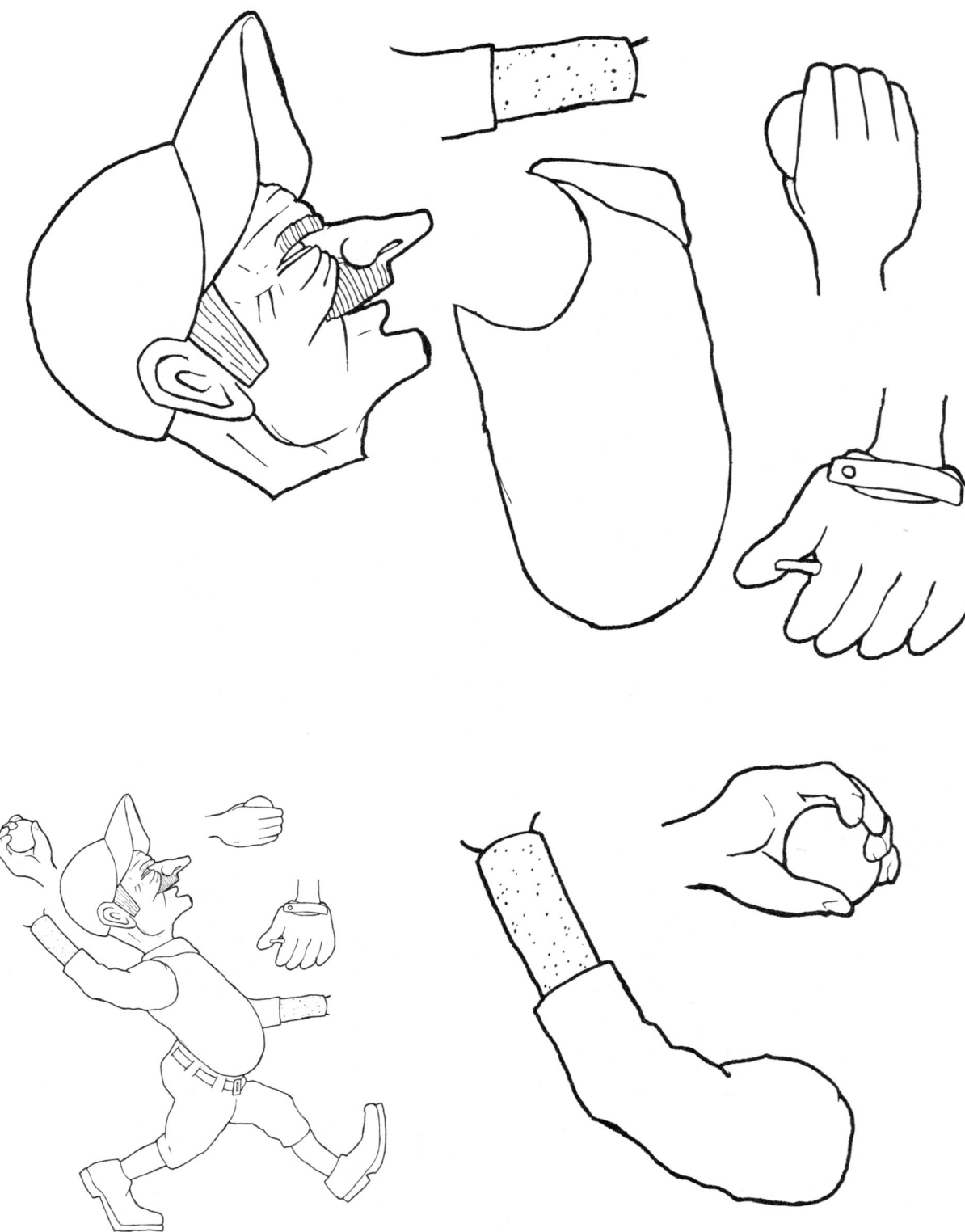

Illus. 54   Patterns for Fireball Feeney.

Illus. 54a (this page and page 54)   Full-scale patterns of Illus. 54.

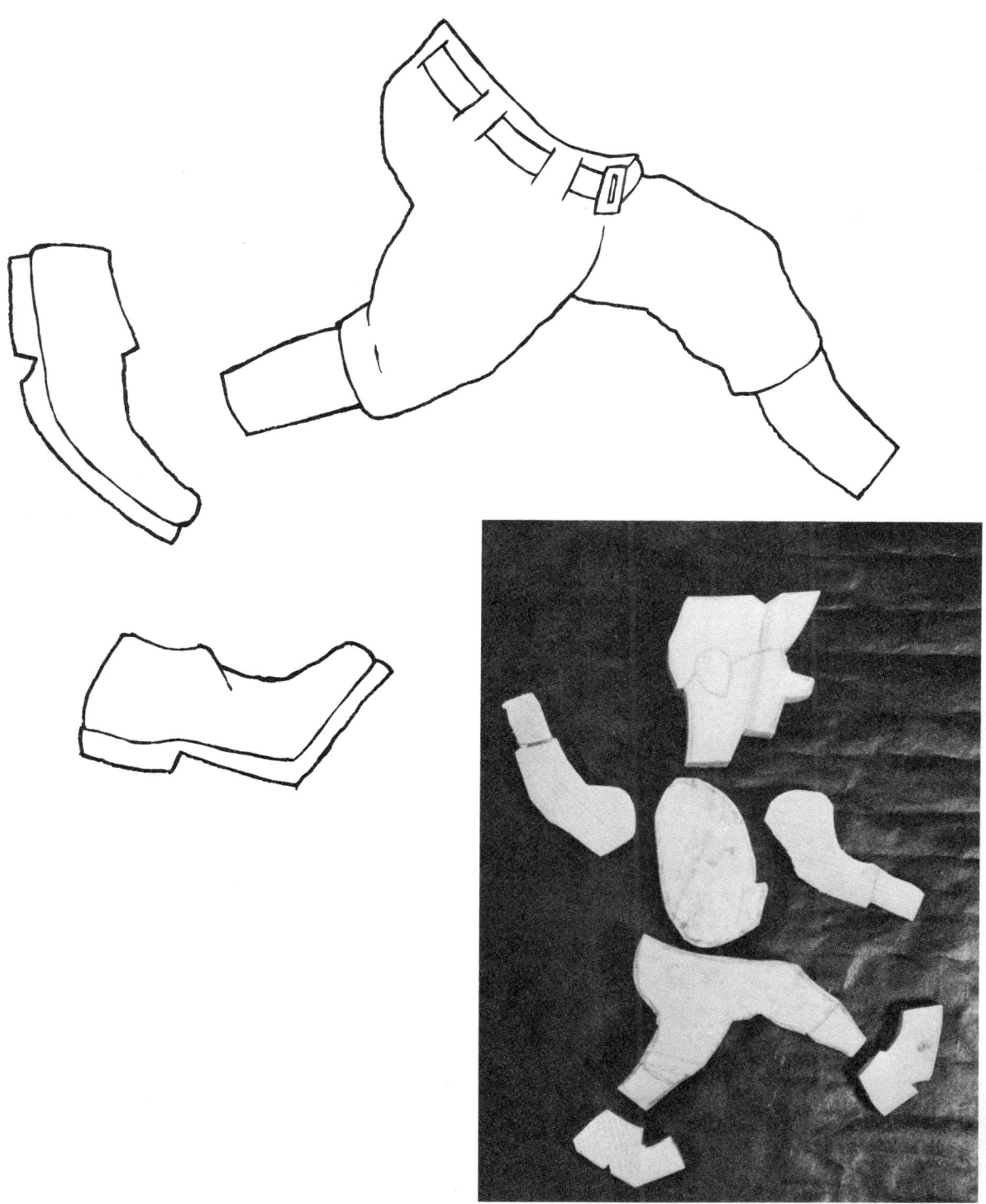

Illus. 55   The various pieces needed to construct Fireball Feeney.

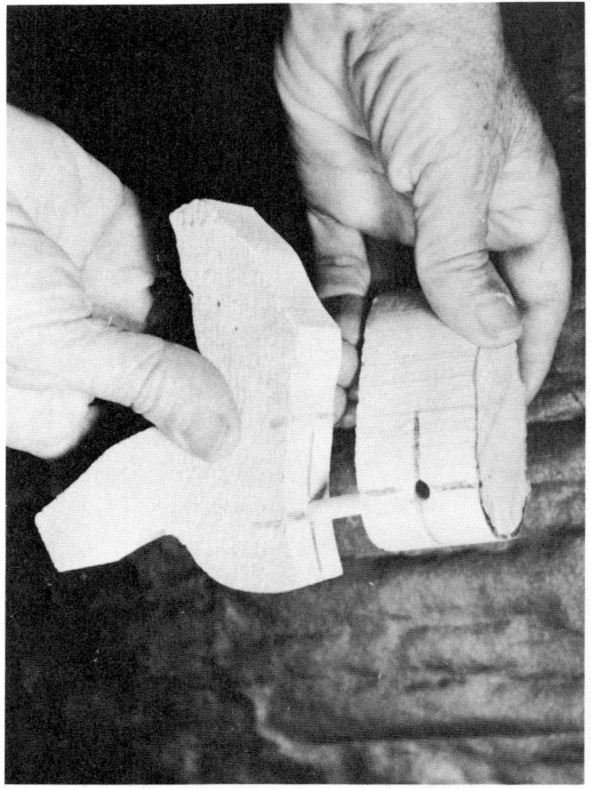

Illus. 56   The upper and lower torsos ready for dowelling and gluing together.

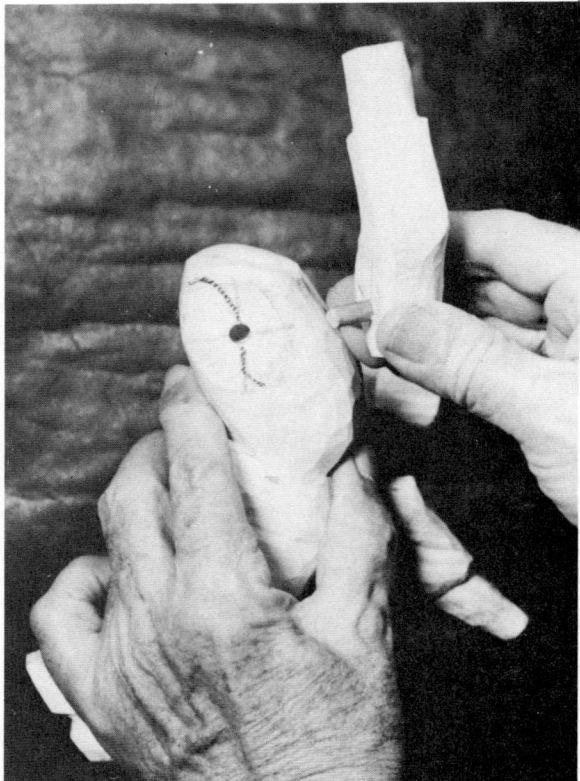

Illus. 57   The arm ready for dowelling and gluing to the upper torso.

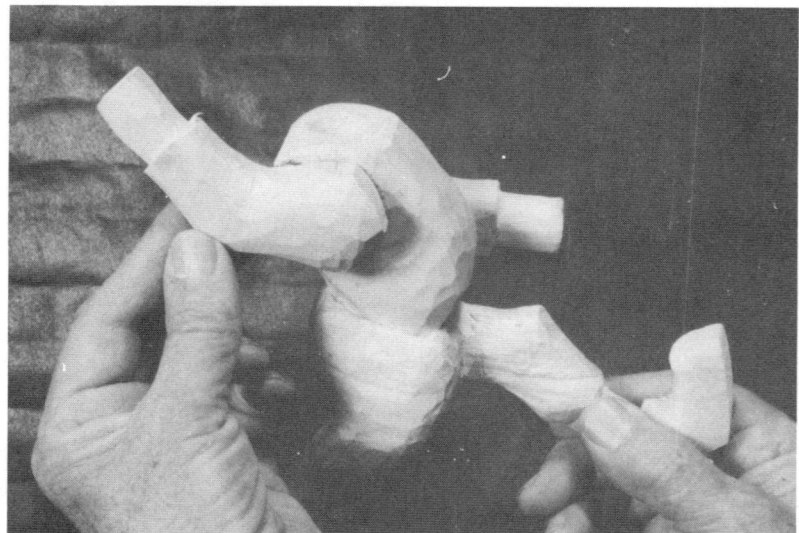

Illus. 58   Positioning the arm before gluing it to the body.

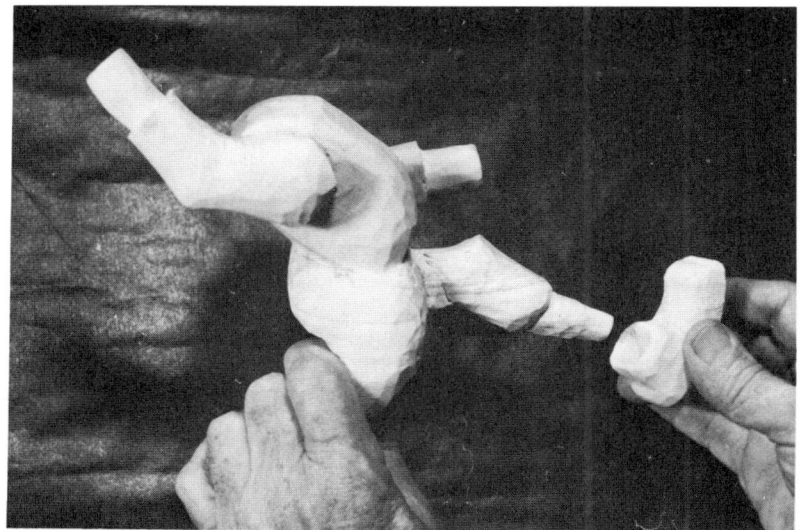
Illus. 59   The shoe ready for gluing to the leg.

Illus. 60   The figure assembled, ready for finishing the carving details.

Bowling Pin Benny

Benny is sometimes called "Gutterball" because of his uncanny habit of rolling the ball down the side gutters.

You will find it easier to carve him if you follow the multipiece carving method described in the project Fireball Feeney. His body and head dimensions are also the same as those for Fireball Feeney. You can either whittle his shoes as part of his legs, or separately, to be attached later. Carve his right hand and the bowling ball from one piece of wood.

FINISHING

Stain his vest mahogany red, trousers medium walnut, hair and shoes Vandyke brown and his bowling ball black. Leave his shirt natural.

Illus. 61   Bowling Pin Benny from the left side.

Illus. 62   Bowling Pin Benny rolls a strike!

Illus. 63   Pattern for Bowling Pin Benny (right side).

Cannonball Bates

Bates's blistering serves ruined many grass and clay courts, so finally, he was restricted to concrete.
1. Whittle his right hand with his racket from one piece of semihard wood.
2. Separately carve his tennis shoes with socks.
3. Whittle his head separately and then his body with the skinny legs. Drill a suitable hole in his body to receive his neck.
4. Drill holes in the tops of his droopy socks to receive his legs.

FINISHING
1. Paint his shirt, socks and tennis balls off-white, his shorts and shoes bright blue and visor green.
2. Paint the soles of his shoes and shirt buttons black.
3. Stain his hair, belt and the handle of his tennis racket dark walnut.

Illus. 64   "Tennis, anyone?"

Illus. 65   Patterns for Cannonball Bates.

Slingin' Shufflebottom, All-American

Shufflebottom is poised to throw his famous "Hail Mary" pass. (This pass, usually a last ditch effort by the quarterback, is thrown long and high in hopes that a team member will catch it or be interfered with in the attempt.)

Carve this project using the multipiece carving method described for Fireball Feeney, keeping in mind that the thickness of the body parts and the head are the same.

1. Carve Shufflebottom's head minus the neck, then glue his head directly onto his shoulders.
2. Whittle the legs and their shoes out of one piece of wood.
3. Join the legs to the body at the knees.
4. Fashion the upper and lower torsos from one piece of wood.
5. After whittling the arms separately, dowel and glue them to the shoulders.

FINISHING

Stain his shirt and socks mahogany red and his pants, shoes and hair dark walnut.

Illus. 67   Slingin' Shufflebottom looking for a receiver.

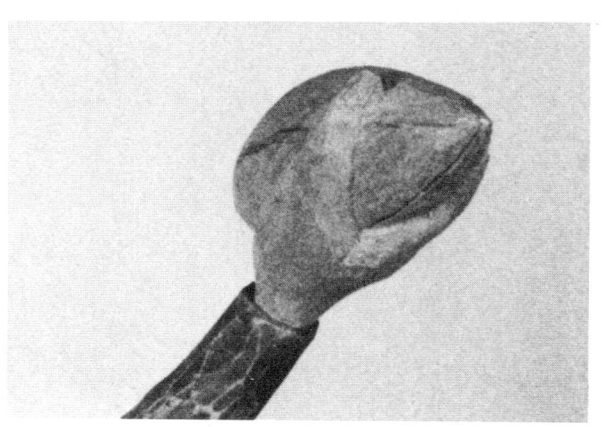

Illus. 66   Detail of Shufflebottom's right hand.

Illus. 68   Left-hand pattern for Slingin' Shufflebottom.

Western Heroes & Heroines

Illus. 69

Stubby

Stubby is more difficult to carve than most of the preceding figures. The position of the hands in the act of rolling a cigarette presents a real challenge. If you follow the step-by-step procedure outlined below, you will find it easier to carve this cowpoke.

1. Trace and transfer the profile view of the body from Illus. 72 to a piece of soft carving wood. Also trace and transfer the pattern of the boot to a separate piece of wood.
2. Trace and transfer the front view from Illus. 72 to the same piece of wood.
3. Band-saw out the front view first. Start sawing at the shoulders, but stop cutting before you reach the end of the legs. Saw out the area between the legs.
4. Now saw out the profile view (Illus. 73). This shows you the body blocked out, ready for carving.
5. Rough out the sides and rear of the arms (Illus. 74).
6. Saw out the boots and carve them to completion before gluing and nailing them to the ends of the legs with small nails, as shown in Illus. 75. Countersink the nails.
7. Rough out the inside of the chaps (Illus. 76).
8. After the body is roughed out, finish carving it (Illus. 70 and 71).

CARVING THE HEAD AND THE HAT

Use separate and different types of wood for the hat and the head. This method allows you to use any piece of wood for the hat and a good piece of semihard carving wood for the face. After you finish carving the hat and the head, dowel and glue them together.

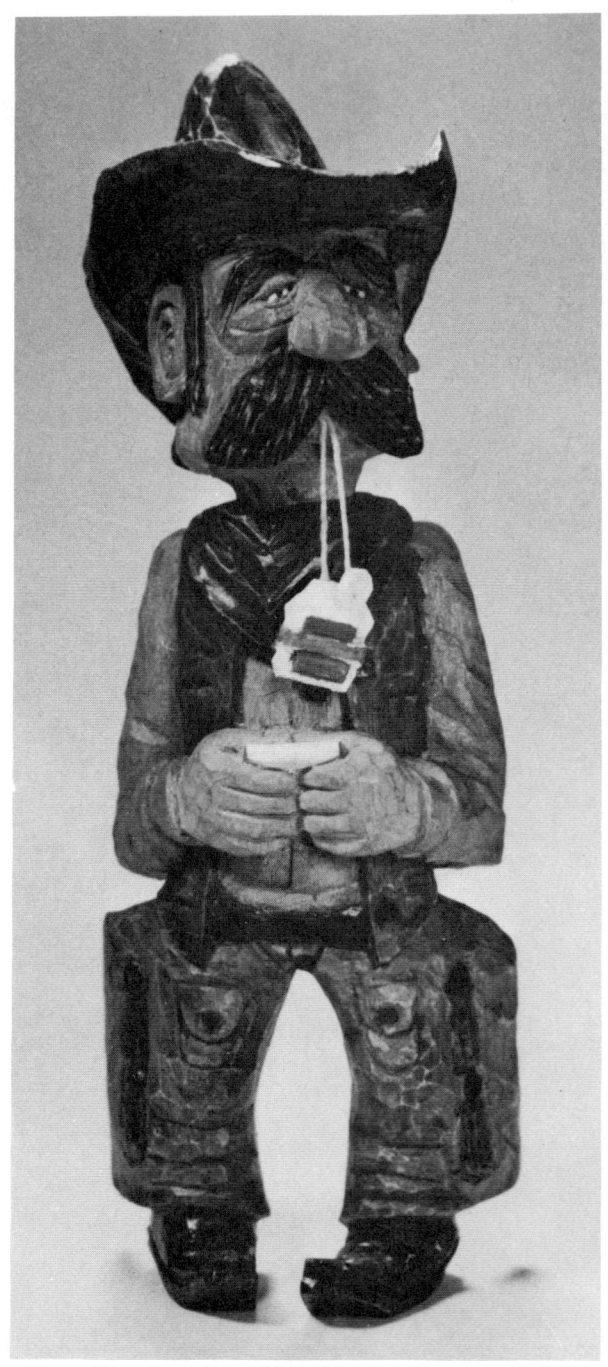

Illus. 70 Stubby rolling his own.

Illus. 71   A rear view of Stubby.

I used the same roughing-out process for the hats for all the western figures included in this book. My process is described below:

1. Trace and transfer the profile view of the face to a semihard piece of good carving wood. Transfer the hat pattern to a separate piece of wood. After sawing them out, hold the crown of the head against the underside of the hat brim to make certain they fit properly (Illus. 77). If they do not fit snugly, glue the hat and the head together with a small amount of glue. After allowing sufficient time for the glue to set, resaw between the crown of the head and the hat brim to ensure a close fit.

2. Carve the head and face to completion.

3. Use a coping saw to block out the crown of the hat as shown in Illus. 78.

4. Rout out the brim of the hat (Illus. 79).

5. Use a gouge and a knife to complete the final shaping of the hat.

6. Dowel and glue the head to the hat. Press them together in a vise until the glue dries.

FINISHING

1. Clean, seal and wax the parts to be stained.

2. Stain the chaps medium walnut and the hat, bandanna, belt, buttons, hair and moustache Vandyke brown. Then, stain the vest and the chap ties mahogany red. Leave the shirt natural wood color.

3. A final light sanding of the stained areas and Stubby is ready for display.

Illus. 72 Patterns for Stubby.

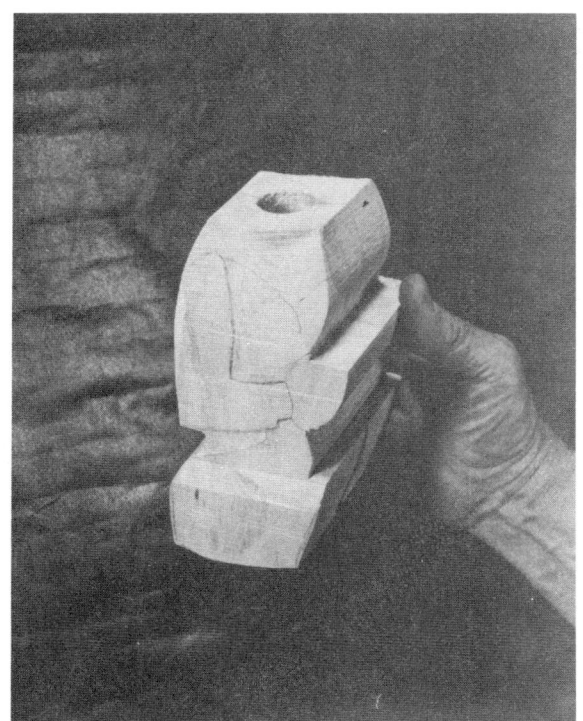
Illus. 73 Stubby's body blocked out.

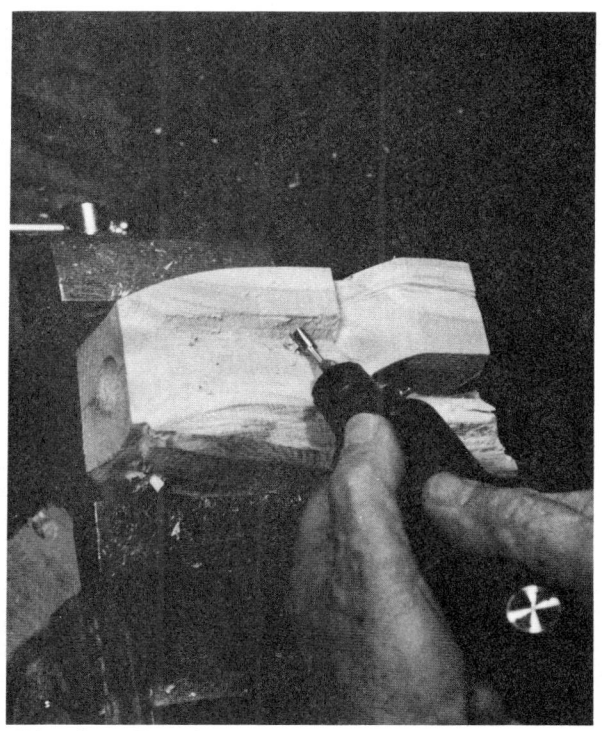
Illus. 74 Routing out around the arms.

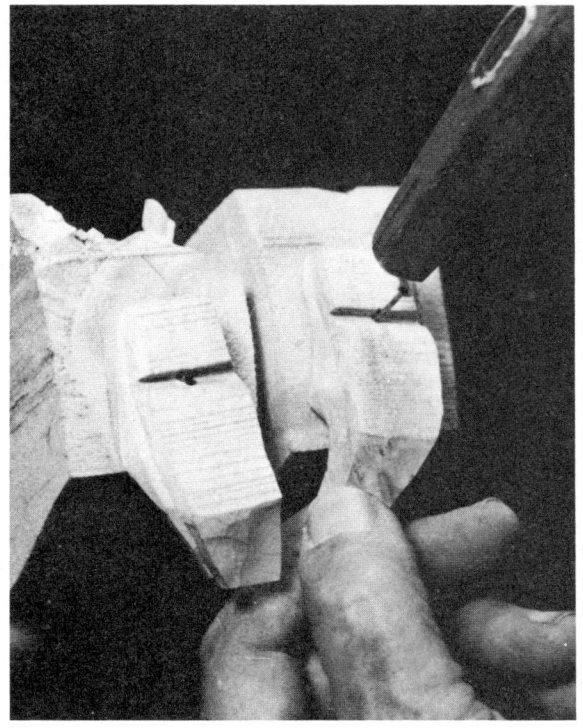
Illus. 75 Nailing the boots to the legs.

Illus. 76 Routing out the inside of the chaps.

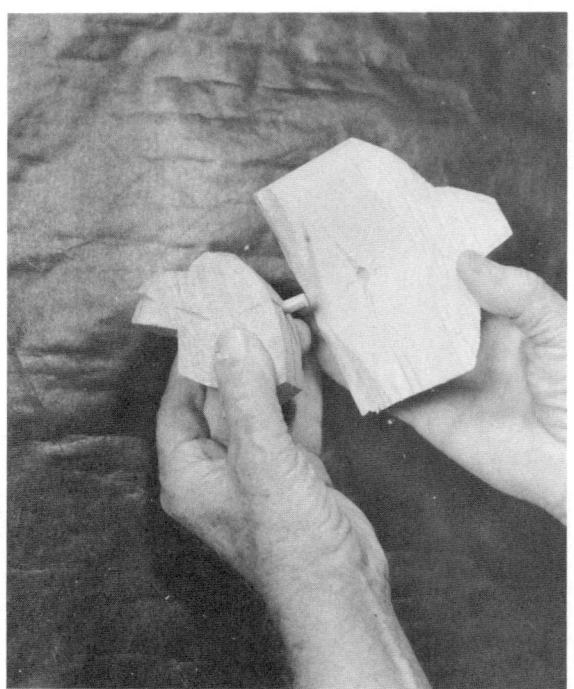

Illus. 77   Head and hat cut to fit.

Illus. 78   Blocking out the crown of the hat with a coping saw.

Illus. 79   Routing out the brim.

Slim, Jim & Tim

By carving cowboys, I can compensate for one of my unfulfilled desires—to have enjoyed the experience of living on the range.

Use the pattern for Slim (Illus. 84) for all three cowpokes included in this section. In each instance, their heads and bodies were whittled separately. The rest of the figure, however, was carved from one piece of wood.

I hope you will enjoy doing these cowboys as much as I did. Just follow the patterns and the photos and you should create some unique characters.

As for the finishing, use your own colorful imagination to decorate these cowpokes.

Illus. 80 Slim and his friends.

Illus. 81 Slim.

Illus. 82 Jim.

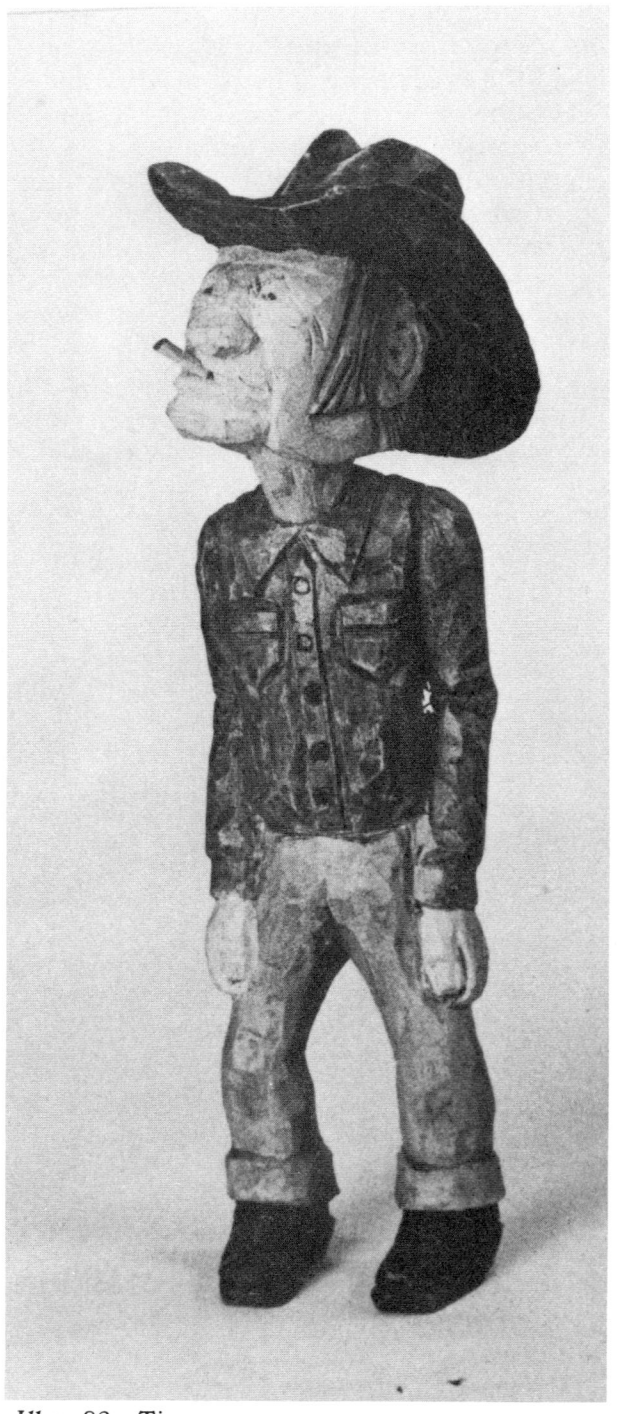

Illus. 83 Tim.

Illus. 84   Patterns for Slim. Use the same patterns for Jim and Tim.

Calamity Jean

Despite her rather innocent expression, this cowgirl has frequently lived up to her title. Her rifle makes men sit up and take notice. It's her equalizer.

Once again, the multipiece carving method for Fireball Feeney aided me in creating Jean. This technique will allow you, also, to use wood scraps that otherwise may be burned in your fireplace.

Using the multipiece carving method, saw out the following parts separately: hat, head, arms, hands, body in two parts (upper and lower torso), boots with the legs and, finally, the gun.

It is simple to partially whittle the above parts, assemble them and finish carving the figure as depicted in Illus. 85. Stain and paint her to suit your own whims.

Illus. 85   Calamity Jean.

Illus. 86   Patterns for Calamity Jean.

Uncle Bub

I whittled this colorful character in remembrance of my favorite relative, Uncle Bub, alias "Skimmerhorn" (his drinking moniker). Drunk or sober he could ride anything on four legs. He was a true representative of the Old West.

For this project, I whittled his lariat separately from his hand. You can use the same method. Then, divide the lariat crosswise into two halves with a jeweller's saw. After drilling a suitable hole between the thumb and forefinger of his left hand, insert the narrow ends of the rope through this hole and glue them together. This method is sometimes easier than fashioning the hand and lariat from one piece of wood.

FINISHING
Paint Uncle Bub's shirt pale pink and his jeans a faded blue color like denim. Stain his hair dark brown, his hat and boots Vandyke brown and the rope a light tan color.

Illus. 87   Looking for a critter to rope and ride.

Illus. 88   Patterns for Uncle Bub.

Noodle Nose Nelson

If you have successfully carved the preceding figures in this book, Noodle Nose will not be too difficult. His oversized proboscis naturally inspired his nickname.

You can carve his gun as part of his hip or whittle it separately and glue it in place. To take advantage of the wood grain running lengthwise with his boots, also whittle them separately and then glue them to his legs.

From this project to the final one in this book I shall not include the finishing section. By now, you should be able to finish the figures to suit yourself, or look through directions under General Finishing (page 13) for a refresher course.

Illus. 89   Noodle Nose Nelson.

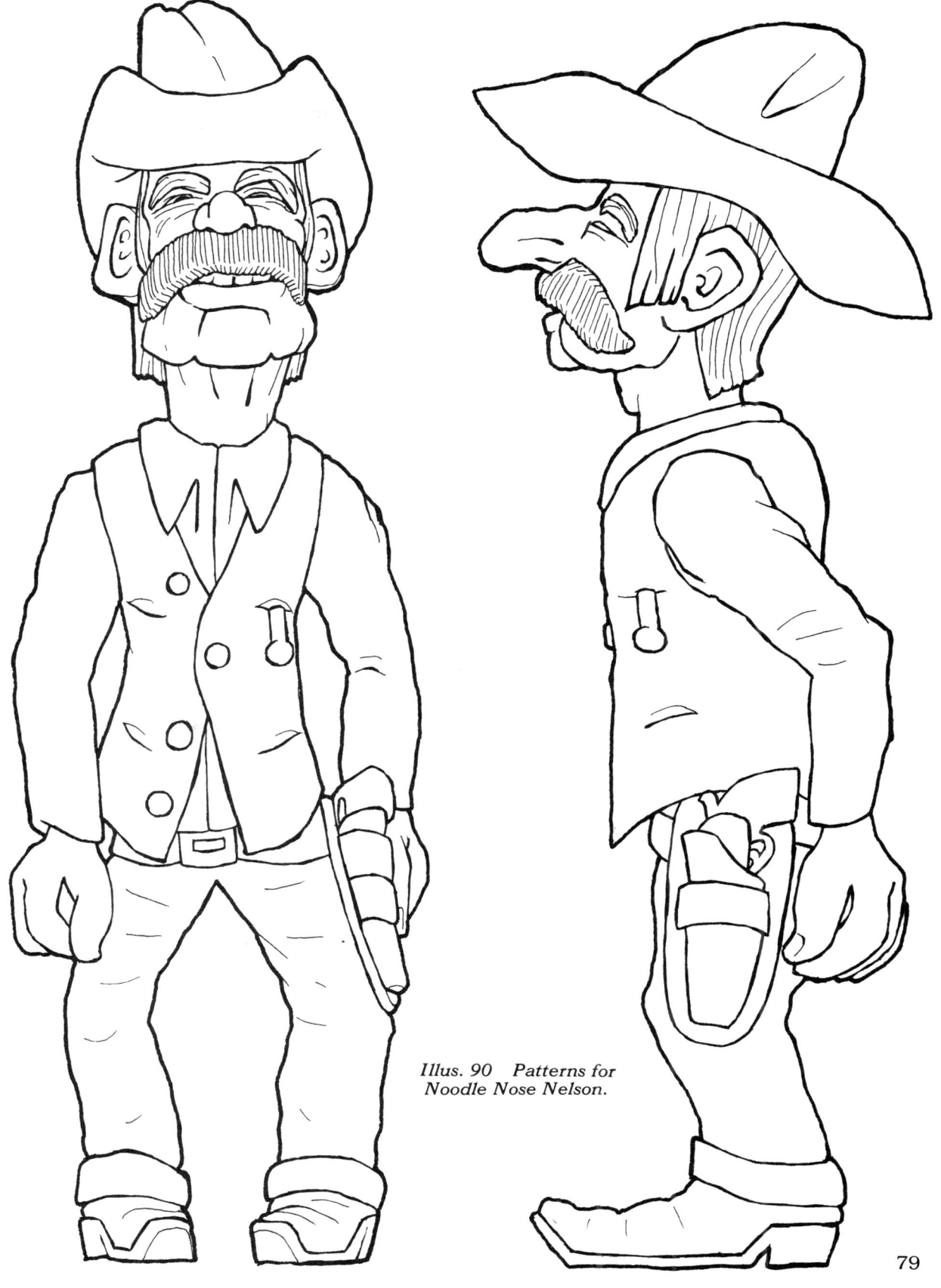

Illus. 90   Patterns for Noodle Nose Nelson.

Tom, the Toquerville Kid

The procedure for carving Tom is similar to that used for Stubby. Tom is from Toquerville, a unique community near Zion National Park, named for Chief Toquer, leader of an Indian tribe in southern Utah.

In addition to a shooting iron, Tom has a lariat. I used a short length of weaver's warp, a strong twine, for his rope. Any fairly heavy, smooth twine will do.

After you stain and finish Tom, apply several coats of Danish oil to the lariat to serve as a stiffener. You can substitute shellac, lacquer or varnish for Danish oil.

Illus. 91   A side view of Tom.

Illus. 92   Tom, the Toquerville Kid.

Illus. 93   Patterns for Tom, the Toquerville Kid.

Taco Juan & Hamburger Harry

This small Mexican figure should challenge and amuse you. With the exception of his huge sombrero and head, Taco Juan was carved from a single piece of wood.

When I whittled his American counterpart—Hamburger Harry (Illus. 94)—I used the same pattern (Illus. 96). I varied the position of his left hand and made him a new suit and hat.

Illus. 94   Hamburger Harry.

Illus. 95   Taco Juan.

Illus. 96   Patterns for Taco Juan.

Patch

A fellow wood-carver served as a model for Patch. He is nicknamed "Patch" because he wears a shield over his eye.

You can either carve his right hand and the lariat from a single piece of wood or whittle the rope and his hand separately, as described in the project Uncle Bub.

Illus. 97   Patch from the back.

Illus. 98   Patch holding his lariat.

Illus. 99 Patterns for Patch.

Bucktooth Bill

Bucktooth Bill, alias "Squirrel Face," is blessed with a prominent set of uppers, his most distinctive feature. I started to whittle a different type of character but got sidetracked into creating him.

Since his hands are hidden in his pockets, you will be spared the task of carving them. For me, hands that are part of the figure are rather difficult to shape properly. When I whittle them separately, however, they are relatively easy.

Bill is another figure that you have the fun of decorating according to your own imagination.

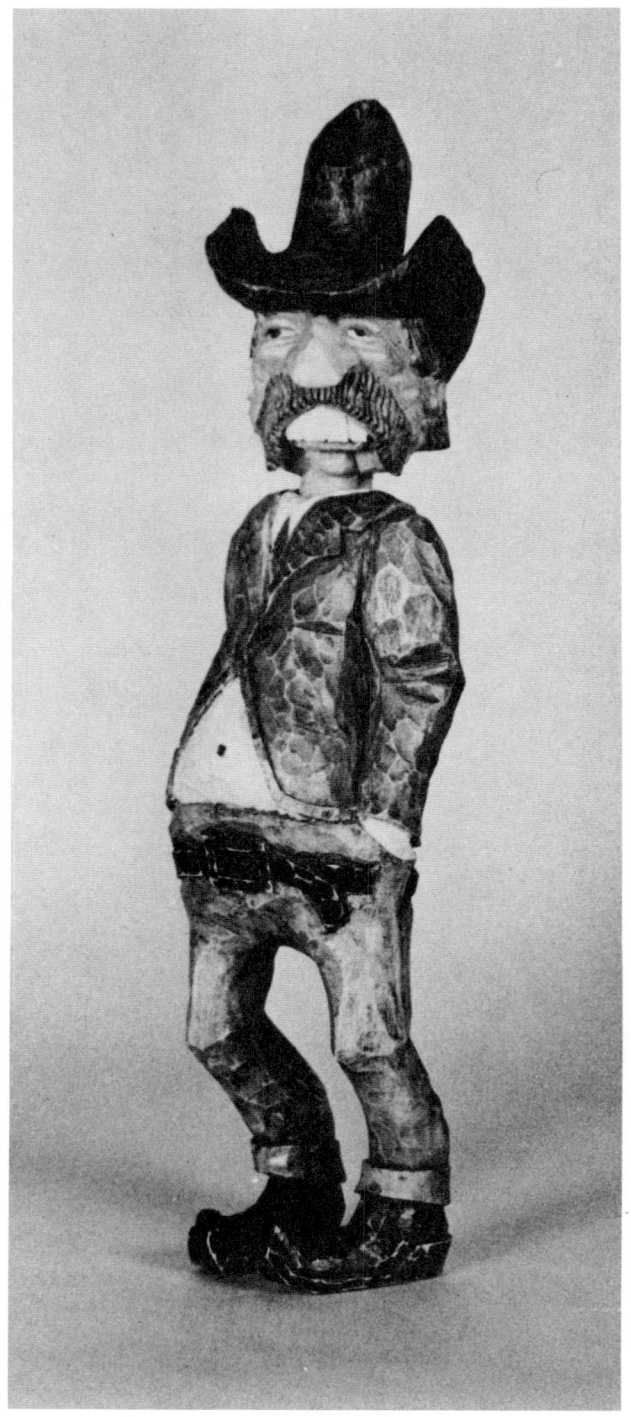

Illus. 100   Bucktooth Bill.

Illus. 101   Patterns for Bucktooth Bill.

Bucktooth Lil

Lil is a friendly, happy girl—a perfect companion for Bucktooth Bill. When they dance, they dance teeth to teeth. Even though she is not a qualified cowgirl, I included her in the western section of this book so she would be near her fiancé, Bucktooth Bill.

I carved her head separately from her body, so that it can be turned in any direction. Also her legs and shoes are whittled separately. Just insert her legs into holes drilled into her shoes and the underside of her body. Her shoes are grossly oversized to provide for good balance.

Illus. 102   Sweethearts.

Illus. 103   Lil and her million-dollar smile.

Illus. 104   Patterns for Bucktooth Lil.

Gunfighters of the Wild West

Illus. 105

Big Ben

Big Ben is really not as mean as he looks. But he assumes this belligerent attitude to frighten his enemies.

Whittling the hands in the holsters may present a problem that was not encountered in the preceding projects. If you follow the procedure outlined below, it should help you to overcome this difficulty.

1. Cut out the arms separately using 1-inch (2.5-cm)-thick wood for each arm. Use the same pattern for both arms. Before partially whittling the arms to shape, drill 7/16-inch (11.11 mm)-diameter holes ½-inch (13-mm) deep in the ends of the arms.
2. Flatten the inner surface of the upper part of the arms and the shoulder sections of the body where the arms are to be attached. I do this flattening on my disc sander.
3. Trace and transfer a pattern of the hand with the pistol holster to a 1½-inch (3.8 cm)-thick piece of semihard carving wood. After sawing the wood to shape, divide the cutout into equal halves. Then flatten the inner surface of each of these halves.
4. Flatten the hip section of the legs to provide a smooth, flat surface for the holster to be glued to later.
5. After partially carving the arms and holsters with their respective hands, dowel and glue the right arm to the body. Next, apply glue to the flat surface of the right hand with its holster and insert the wrist into the sleeve.
6. Allow the glue to set for several minutes, then place the figure in a vise and press the arm firmly against the body.
7. Use C clamps to press the holster against the hip. Wait until the glue has set firmly, then repeat the same process with the left arm and hand.
8. Finish carving the arms, hands and holsters to completion.

Illus. 106   Big Ben, boss among men.

Illus. 107   Patterns for Big Ben.

Fast Draw

Fast Draw was known and feared throughout the Wild West for his lightning-quick draw. Since he was a good sport, he always invited his opponent to draw first.

Refer to the project Big Ben for detailed instructions regarding the placement and whittling of the arms, the hands and their holsters. The left hand, gun and holster are carved from one piece of wood. Whittle the right hand separately and insert it into the right sleeve.

Since the arms are duplicates, transfer the pattern to a 2-inch (5.1-cm)-thick piece of wood and saw it out. Then split the cut-out into equal halves. Complete the arms as explained for Big Ben.

Illus. 108   Fast Draw: "You draw first and you'll never draw again."

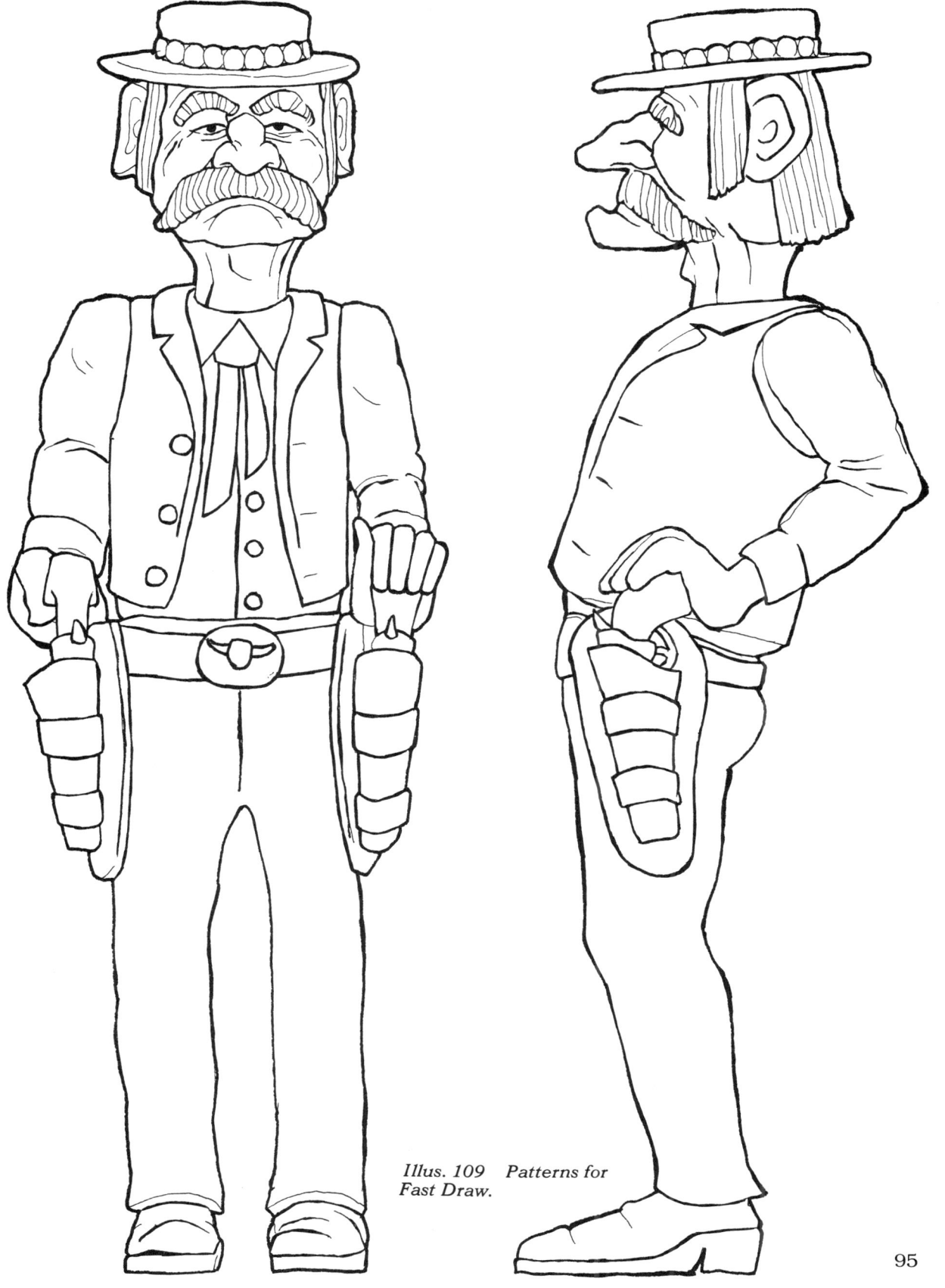

Illus. 109   Patterns for Fast Draw.

Sure Draw

This pleasant gunslinger invariably paralyzes his adversary with the chilling threat—*Gotchamagunsonya!*

His arms are duplicates, cut from the same pattern, as described in directions for Fast Draw. I carved the revolvers and their hands separately, then whittled the arms. Refer frequently to Illus. 110 and 111 for aid in whittling these rather troublesome sections of the gunslinger.

Illus. 110   Sure Draw: "Drop y'ur gun belt or I'll drop you."

Illus. 111   Patterns for Sure Draw.

Shotgun Sam

Sam is seldom seen without his trusty shotgun. He has used it successfully to discourage jailhouse lynchings.

If you have carved the other gunfighters in this book, you should be able to fashion Sam without too much difficulty.

1. It is simpler to whittle his gun and hand separately. After you have finished the gun, cut the gun barrel about 1¼ inches (3.2 cm) from the end.
2. Carve the hand that holds the gun in a closed position (Illus. 114 and 115).
3. Drill a hole large enough to receive both sections of the gun barrel.
4. Stain the shotgun.
5. Apply glue and insert the cut sections of the barrel into the hand (Illus. 116). If you achieve a pressed fit, it will be impossible to detect any cut in the barrel.

Illus. 112   A rear view of Shotgun Sam.

Illus. 113   Sam and his trusty scatter-gun.

Illus. 114   Patterns for Shotgun Sam (front view).

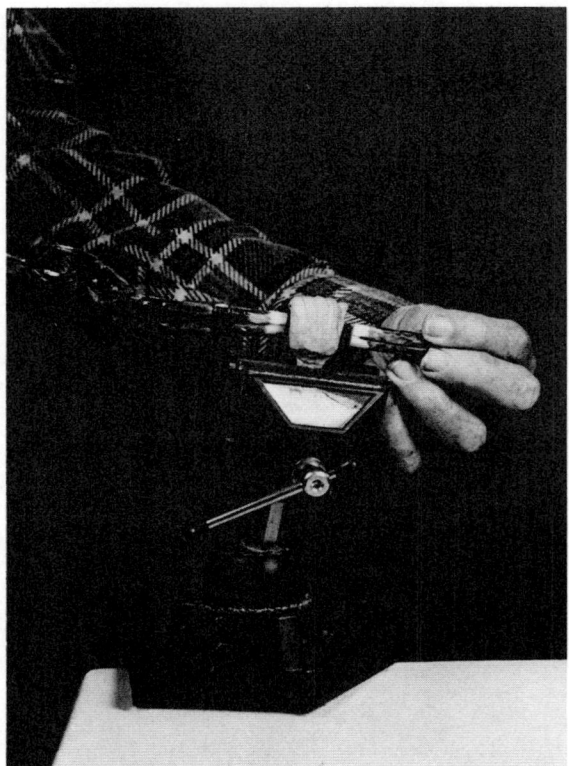

Illus. 116 (above) Inserting the barrel sections into the hand. D-Vise furnished by Dremel Division of Emerson Electric Co.

Illus. 115 Shotgun Sam (side view).

MERRY MUSICIANS

Illus. 117

Cactus Jack, Country Singer

About ten years ago, I whittled Cactus Jack to serve as a caller for a set of square dancers that I created. For this book, Jack kindly consented to assume the role of country singer.

I carved his left hand and his hat out of one piece of avocado wood. If you prefer, do them as two separate pieces following the procedure described for Stubby.

It is easier to whittle the microphone handpiece and its supporting post separately. Drill a 1/16-inch (1.59 mm)-diameter hole in the bottom of the handpiece and a similar hole between the thumb and forefinger of Jack's right hand. The post can then be inserted through Jack's hand and into the handpiece.

Illus. 118   Cactus Jack, country singer.

Illus. 119 Pattern for Cactus Jack (front view).

Illus. 120 Pattern for Cactus Jack (profile view).

Messrs. Sharps & Flats

These two characters, each playing a concertina, were whittled from the same pattern (Illus. 123).

Carve the concertina and the hands out of one piece of wood. Be careful to shape the wrists so they will fit into the sleeve holes.

If you whittle Mr. Sharps first, it is a simple task to carve Mr. Flats. It merely involves the problem of trading jeans and a vest for overalls and a different face.

Illus. 121   Mr. Sharps and his concertina.

Illus. 122   Mr. Flats reaching a high note.

Illus. 123   Patterns for Mr. Sharps and Mr. Flats.

G. Cleff, Choirmaster

G. Cleff is recognized everywhere as the choir director with a bottle. He imbibes between numbers to restore his shaky confidence. Note the classy spats concealing part of his shoes. The huge bow tie adds further distinction to this colorful caricature.

You can either whittle the flask together with his left hand out of a single piece of wood, or separately. Naturally, the latter method is easier.

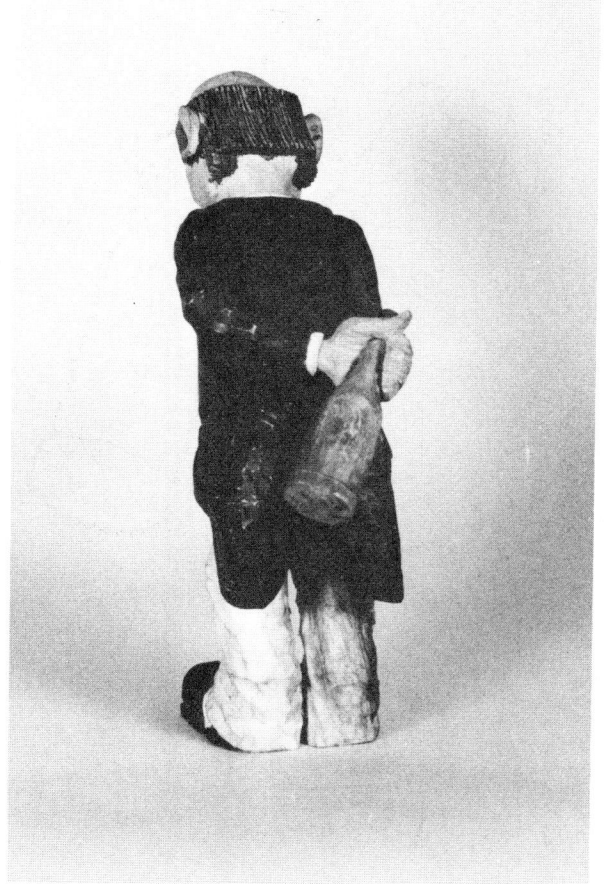

Illus. 124   G. Cleff and his pacifier, the bottle.

Illus. 125   G. Cleff: "You're off-key, Ethel!"

Illus. 126   Pattern for G. Cleff (profile view).

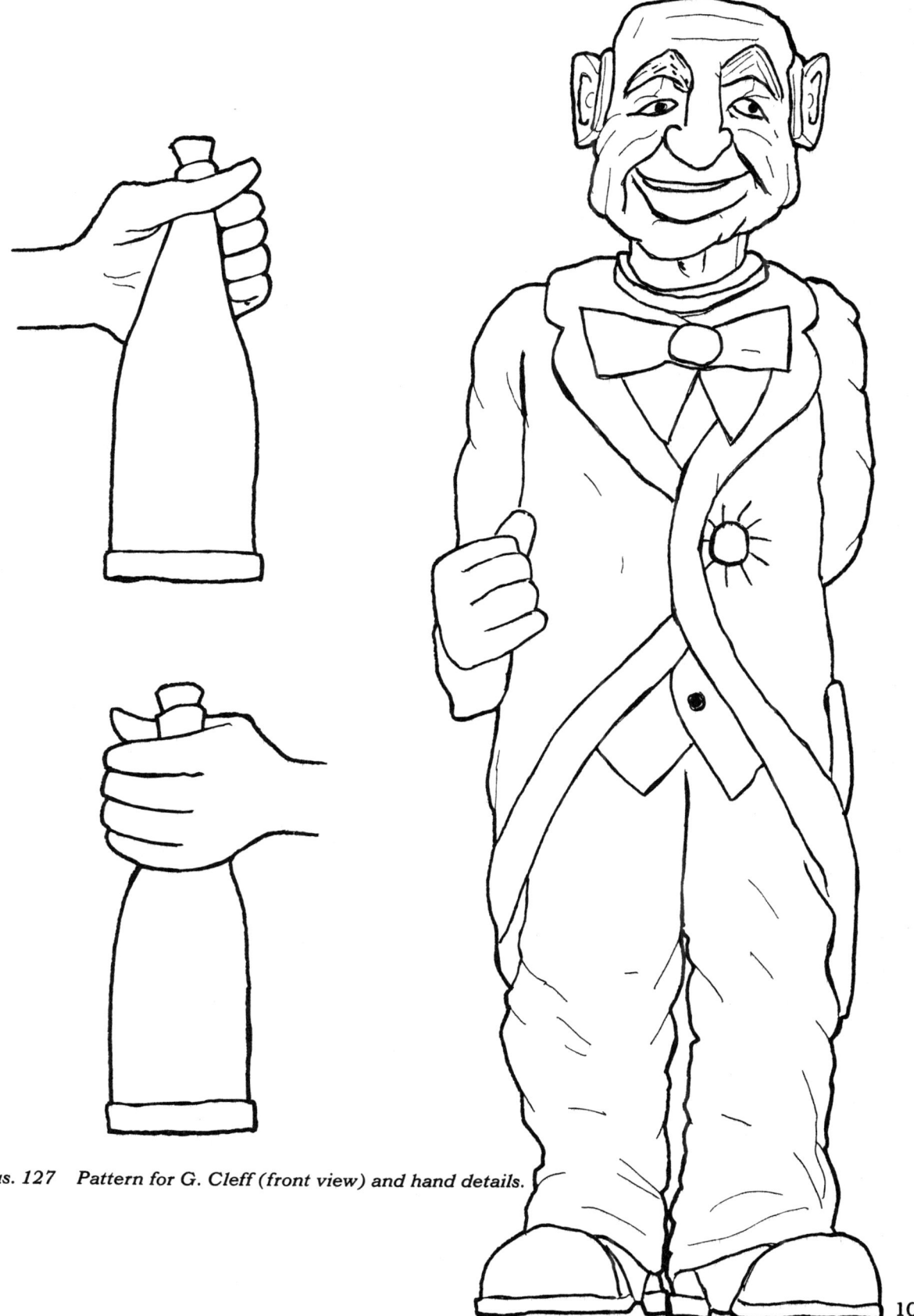

Illus. 127 Pattern for G. Cleff (front view) and hand details.

Banjo Billy

Banjo Billy, a crooning troubadour, seldom fails to draw smiles from his audience. One has to pity the overburdened nag that must transport Banjo Billy to Nashville, however.

Again, I used the multipiece method to carve Billy and his horse (see Fireball Feeney).

1. Divide the upper half of his body from the lower half just above the belt line. Shape the arms and body from the same piece of wood.
2. After roughing out both sections, dowel and glue them together.
3. Then, finish whittling them.
4. Carve the left hand and the banjo from one piece of wood. Insert and glue into the left sleeve.
5. Whittle the right hand separately from another piece of wood. Insert and glue at the correct angle into the right sleeve.
6. Chisel a hole between the hand and the neck of the banjo for the strings to go through. Waxed, heavy thread serves for the banjo strings.
7. Whittle the posts, keys and fittings separately and then add them to the instrument.
8. When you are ready to make the piano stool, use the patterns of the base and the leg as shown in Illus. 134. Trace and transfer the base pattern to a piece of 2¼-inch (5.7-cm)-thick piece of wood. Make certain the grain runs perpendicular to the length of the legs. If the grain runs horizontal, the wood is easily broken.

Illus. 128 Banjo Billy: "Nashville, here I come!"

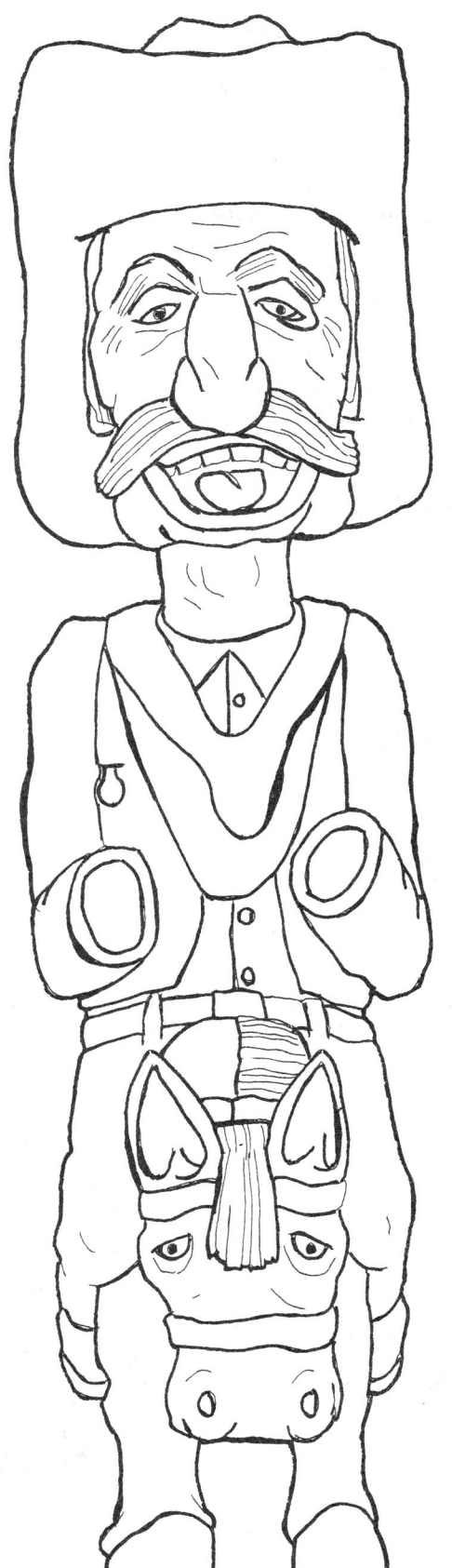
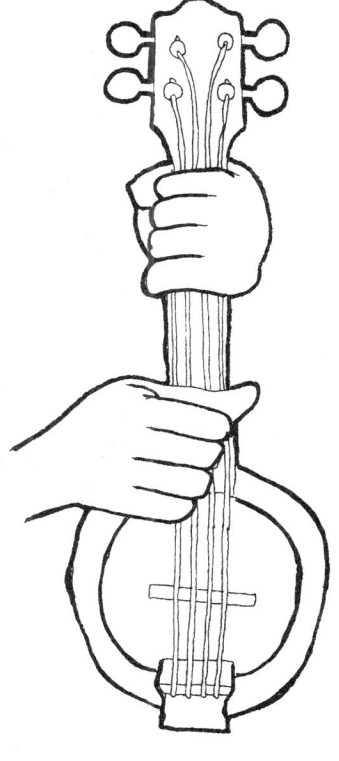

Illus. 129 Pattern for Banjo Billy (front view).

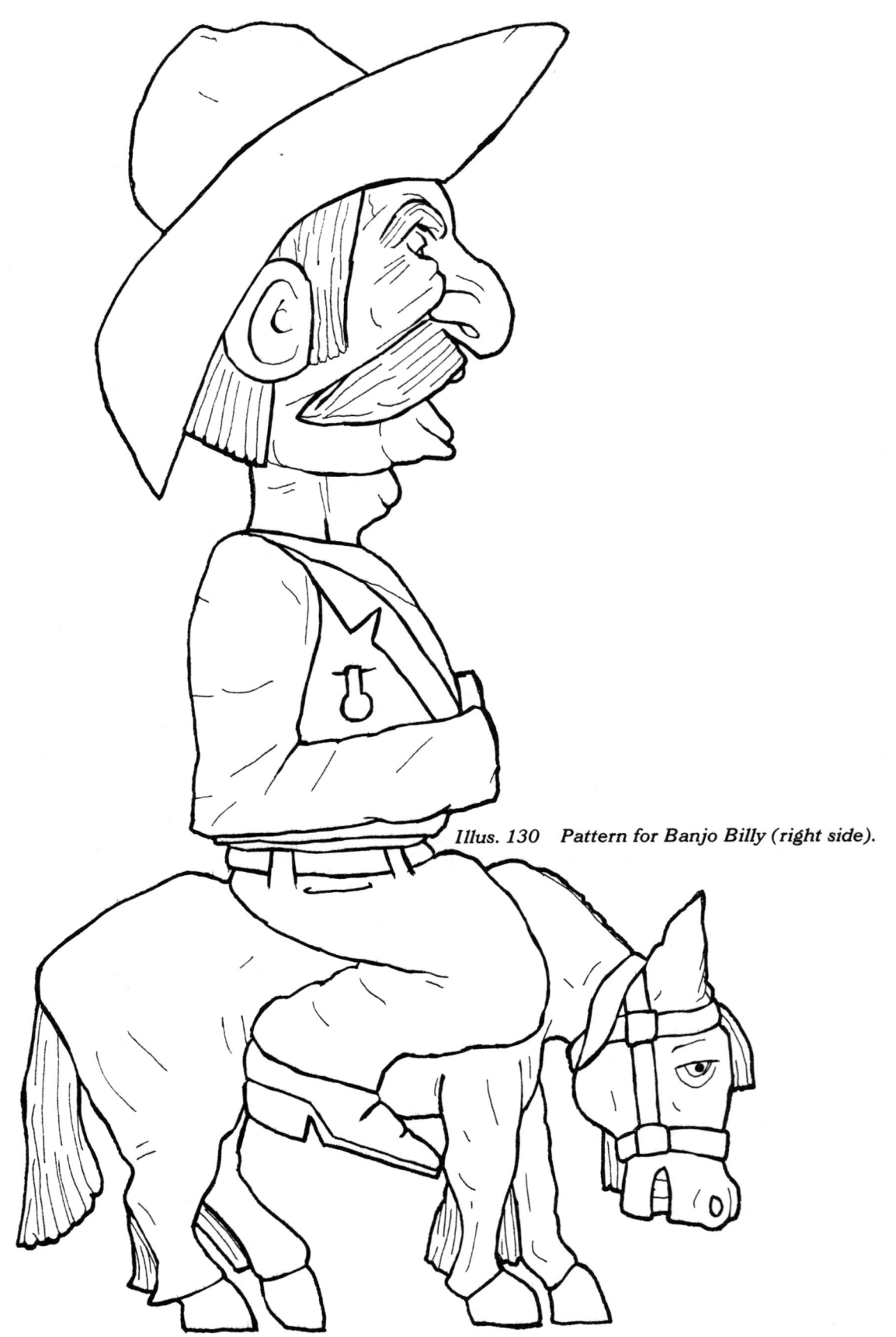

Illus. 130   Pattern for Banjo Billy (right side).

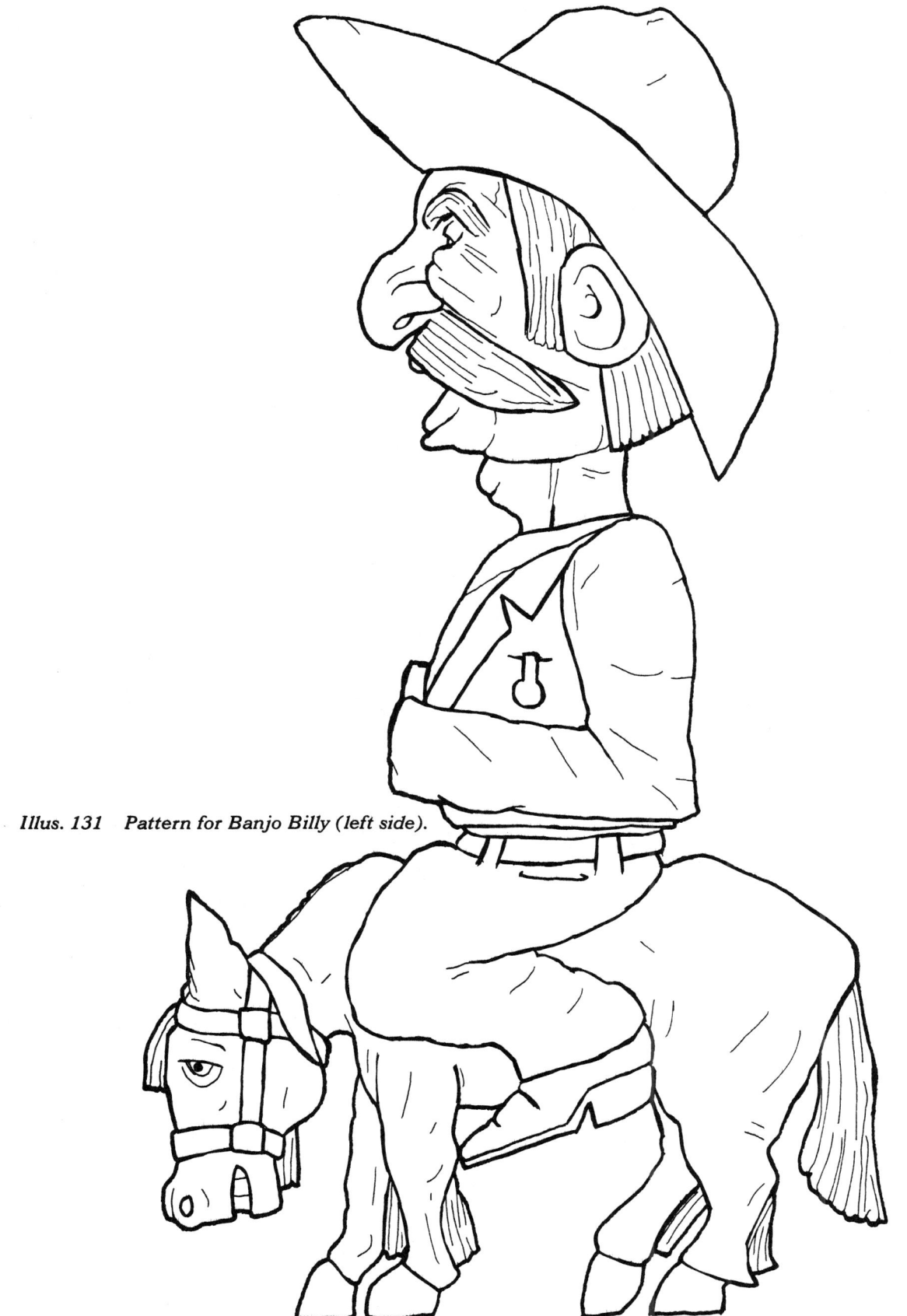

Illus. 131 Pattern for Banjo Billy (left side).

Professor Higginsniffer

This concert pianist and his baby grand are an attractive pair. Often they inspire exclamations of surprise and delight from their captive audience.

1. Partially whittle the lower torso and the piano stool seat from one piece of wood.
2. Carve the button shoes with their ankles and join them to the Professor's legs.
3. Shape the upper torso with its arms from a separate piece of wood.
4. Dowel and glue together both parts of the body.
5. As soon as the glue dries, finish whittling the entire body minus the hands.
6. Whittle the hands separately from another piece of wood. Then attach the hands to the arms.
7. Fit the head loosely to the shoulders so it can be turned in any desired direction.
8. When you are ready to make the piano stool, use the patterns of the base and the leg as shown in Illus. 134. Trace and transfer the base pattern to a piece of 2¼-inch (5.7-cm)-thick piece of wood. Make certain the grain runs perpendicular to the length of the legs. If the grain runs horizontally, the wood is easily broken.
9. After you saw out the base, use the pattern of the stool leg as a template to outline the shape of the legs. I used a coping saw to rough out these items and a whittling knife to finish them. You can use the same equipment.
10. Then you can dowel and glue the finished base to the piano seat and Professor Higginsniffer.

Illus. 132 Professor Higginsniffer.

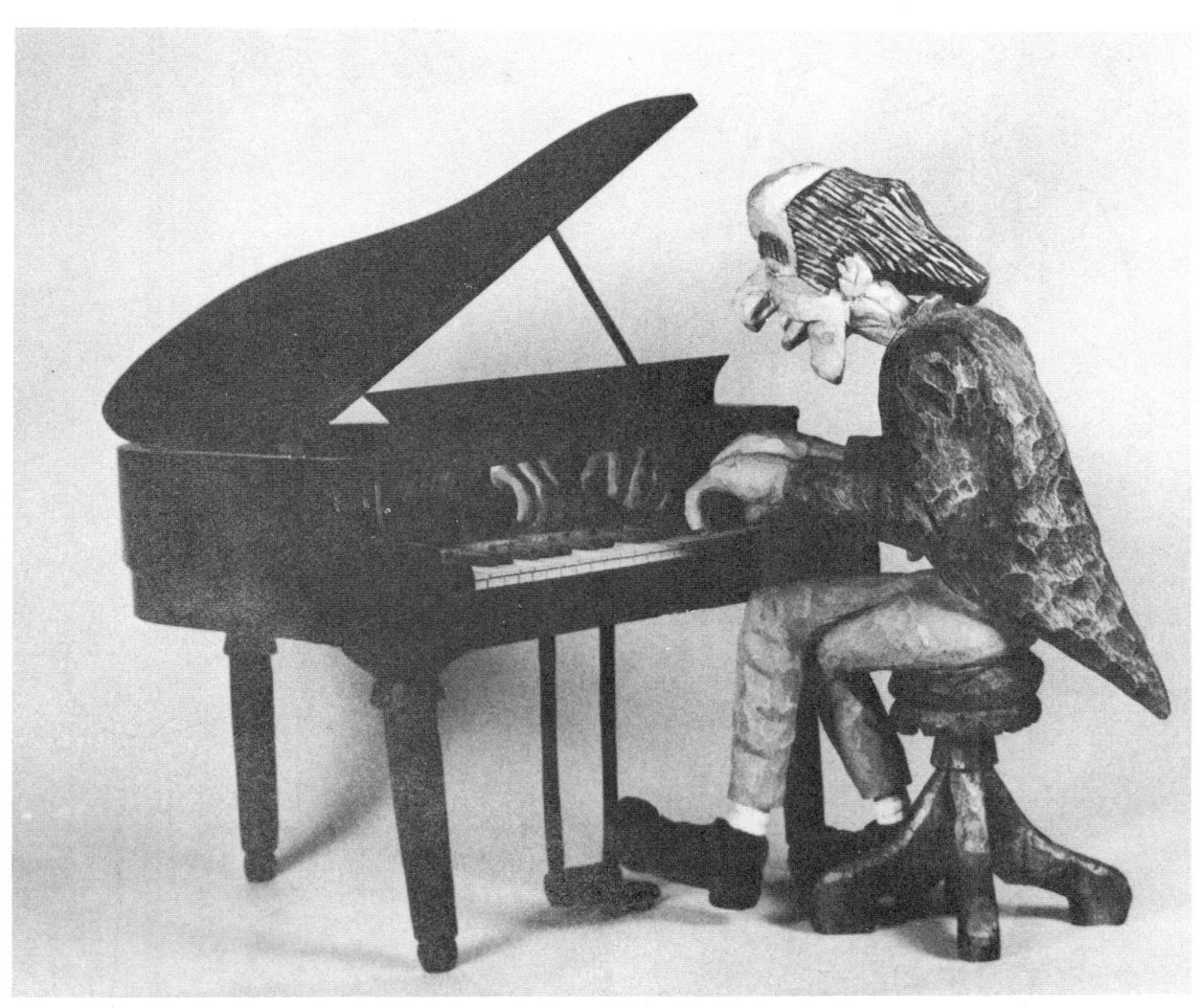
Illus. 133 The Professor playing his interpretation of Chopin's "Polonaise."

Illus. 134 Pattern for Professor Higginsniffer (front view).

BASE OF STOOL AND LEG ACTUAL SIZE

Illus. 135 Pattern for Professor Higginsniffer (left side).

The Baby Grand

Friends ask me, "Did you carve the piano?" My answer is, "No, I did not carve the entire instrument. I only whittled the legs and the pedals. I used a band-saw and a jigsaw to fashion the rest of the piano."

The plans provided for this project and the directions given below should enable you also to build this piano:

1. Trace and transfer the pattern of the body frame (Illus. 138) to a 1¾-inch (4.4-cm)-thick piece of wood and be sure to *double* the size of the pattern. (Since I did not have a large enough piece, I glued scraps together to produce a piece of sufficient size to accommodate the body pattern.)

Saw out the inside of the body pattern first and then the outside to form a frame.

2. Trace and transfer to a ¾-inch (1.9-cm)-thick piece of wood a pattern of the bottom, or floor, of the piano as shown in Illus. 139. Also, *double* the size of this pattern. Saw out the bottom and glue it to the body frame. Drill five ³⁄₁₆-inch (4.76 mm)-diameter holes into the floor. Refer to Illus. 139 for the location of these holes.

3. Close off the front opening of the piano frame with a ½-inch (1.3-cm)-thick piece of wood 1½ inches (3.8 cm) wide by 7⅜ inches (18.8 cm) long.

4. Cut out and shape the legs as shown in Illus. 140. You can either turn them to shape on a miniature lathe or whittle them to the form shown in Illus. 140 or to a shape of your own design. I dowelled the legs loosely into the floor of the piano so they could be removed when desired. The pattern of Professor Higginsniffer was designed to fit the pattern of the piano. If you need to make adjustments on the legs and the height of the piano keyboard (steps 9 and 10), use the finished carving of the Professor as your guide.

5. Shape the pedals and suspend them from the underside of the piano with ³⁄₁₆-inch (4.76-mm)-diameter posts. These can also be attached loosely for easy removal.

6. Now, cut out the following parts: the lid or top of the piano (Illus. 141); the music support (Illus. 142) and the two brackets that fit on either end of the keyboard (Illus. 138), but read step 8 before cutting.

7. Sand all of these parts, then spray them with several coats of flat black paint. Sand lightly between coats.

8. For the keyboard, use a ³⁄₁₆-inch (4.76-mm)-thick piece of semihard white wood 1¼ inches (3.2 cm) wide by 6¼ inches (15.8 cm) long. Then, mark off the ¼-inch (.6-cm) white keys with a pencil. Carefully saw almost through these lines with a fine saw blade. A jigsaw or coping saw is suitable for making these fine cuts that separate the white keys. If you do not plan to use a piece of plastic mirror as suggested in step 10, then add ⅛ inch (.3 cm) to the length of the white and black keys. Also, add ⅛ inch (.3 cm) to the end brackets mentioned in step 6.

9. Cut small pieces of wood for the black keys as shown in Illus. 138. Stain or paint these keys black. When they are dry, glue them in place on the keyboard.

10. If you have a piece of ⅛-inch (.3-cm)-thick plastic mirror, cut it to the correct size and fasten it to the front of the piano. Next, glue the end brackets in place and also the keyboard.

11. Glue the sheet music holder in place. Attach the top or lid of the piano to the frame with small brass hinges.

12. Make the lid support bracket as shown in Illus. 141. Stain or paint it black and glue it to the inside of the piano box.

The above instructions are merely guides and suggestions. If you wish to change them, do not hesitate to do so. It is very possible that you will design a better piano.

Illus. 136   The finished baby grand.

*Illus. 137   A drawing of the piano assembled.
Drawing by Jerald Tolman.*

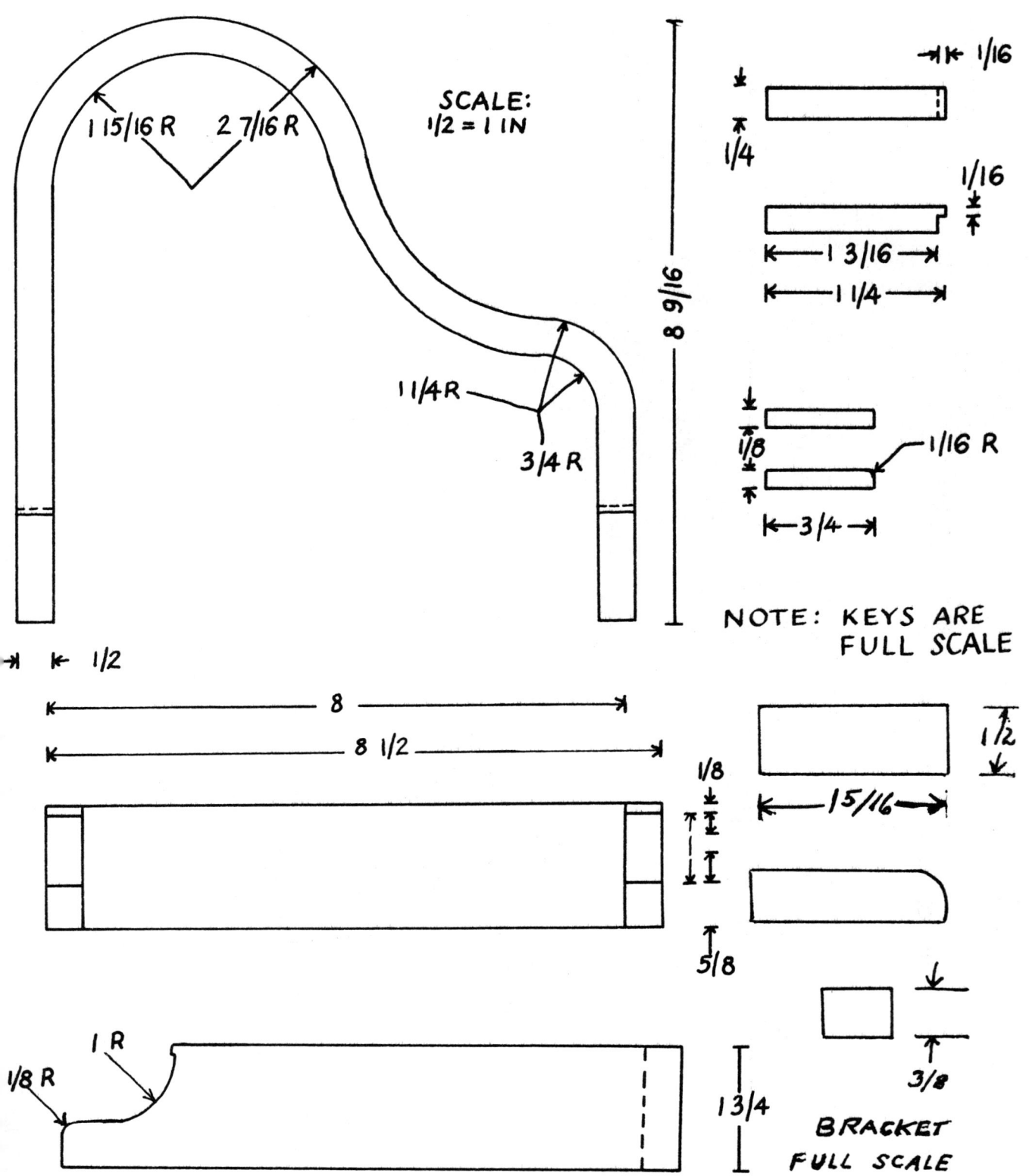

Illus. 138 Scale drawings of the frame, the keys and the sides of the piano.

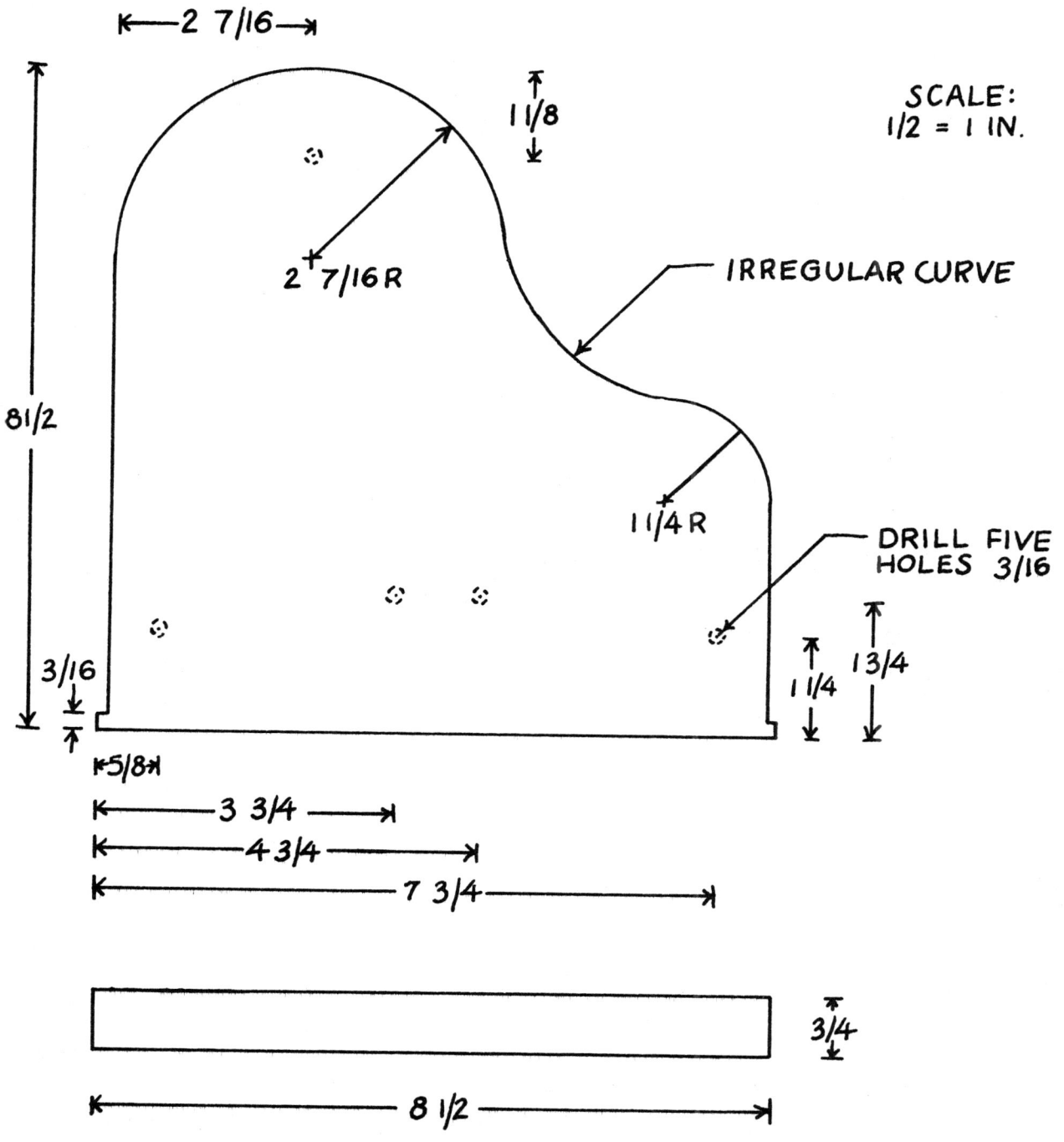

Illus. 139 Scale drawing of the bottom of the piano.

121

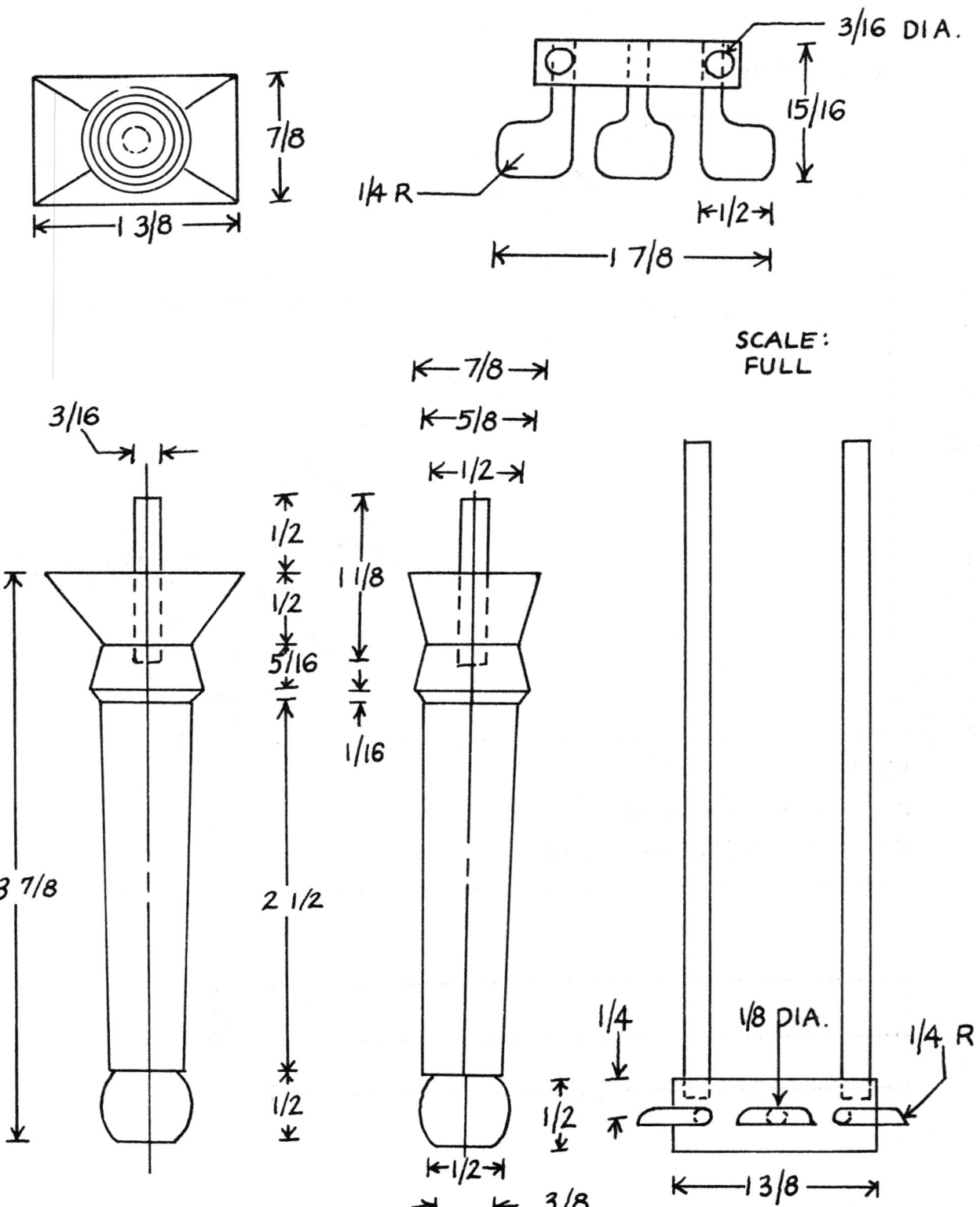

Illus. 140 Full-scale drawings of the legs and pedals.

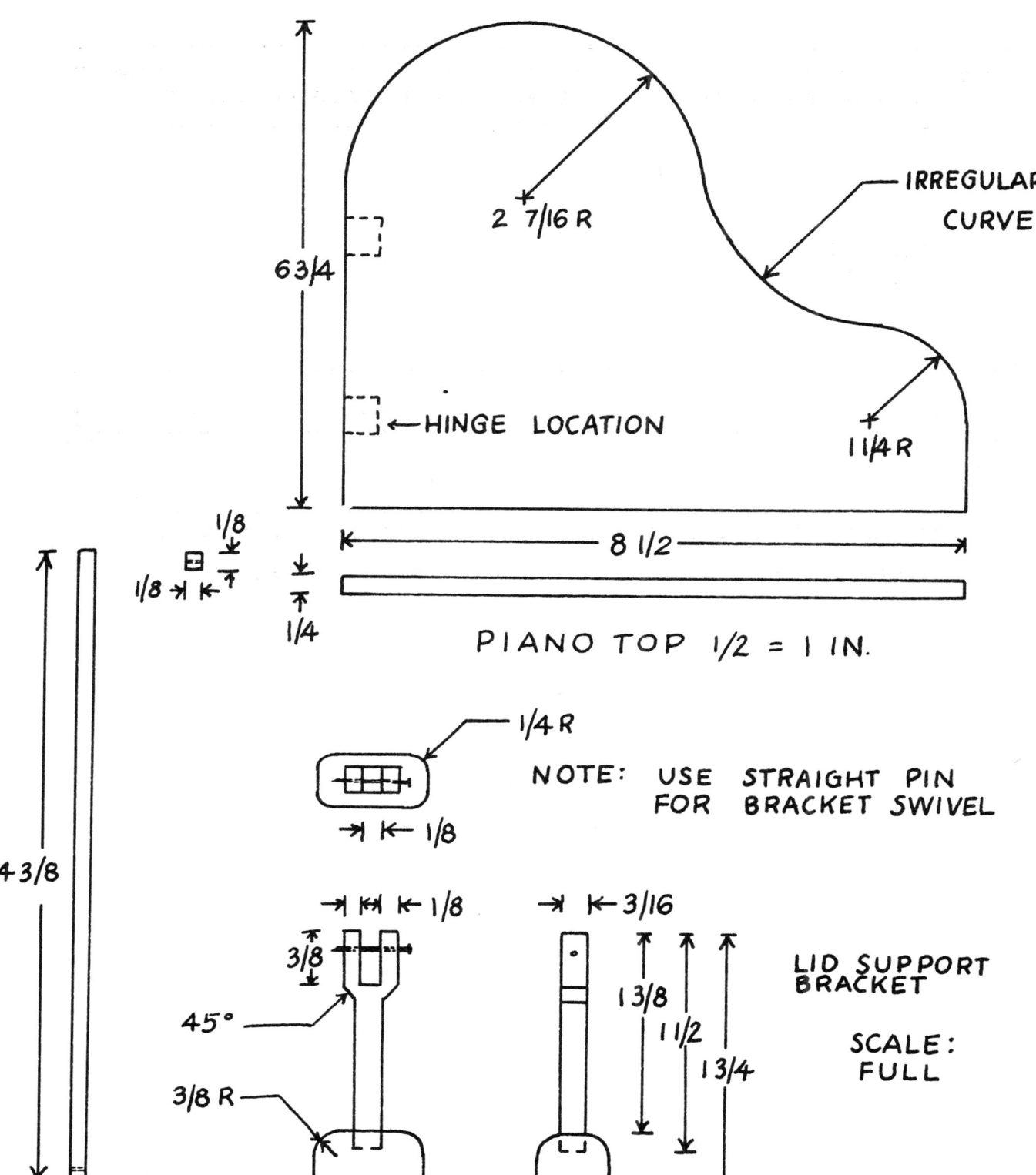

Illus. 141   Plans for the piano top and its support.

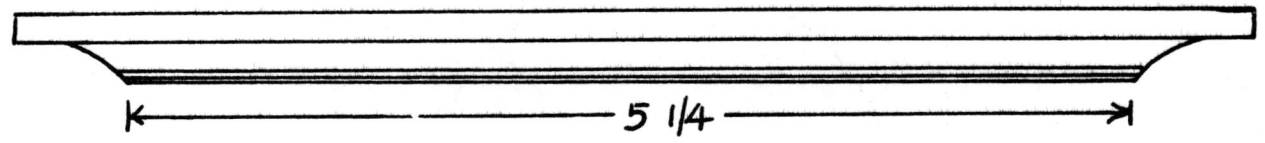

SCALE: FULL

Illus. 142   Picture frame moulding used for the music support (the style is optional).

Illus. 143   The virtuoso at the keyboard.

ABOUT THE AUTHOR

Bill Higginbotham, born and raised in Utah, graduated from Brigham Young University with high honors and went on to teach arts and crafts for 29 years in Utah and California. He passed on to his students his enormous enthusiasm for whittling. "I taught many crafts, but the only craft that really captured my imagination was woodcarving. It is the only one that offers a real challenge. It is the least taught craft in schools of America," he says. Bill Higginbotham has appeared on national television programs and, in addition to whittling and writing books, enjoys swimming. He and his wife, Frances, divide their time between their farm, in Toquerville, Utah, and home in St. George, Utah. They have three children and 11 grandchildren.

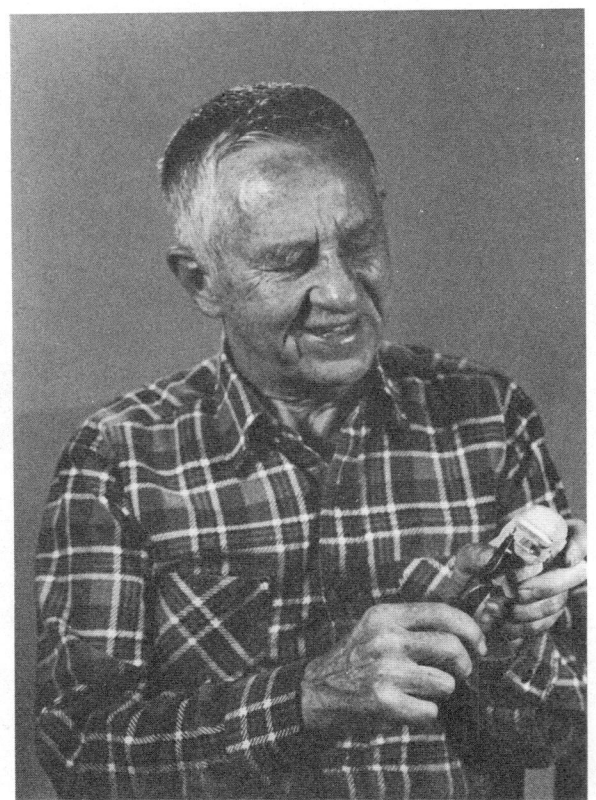

"Whittlin' Bill" Higginbotham enjoying himself.

INDEX

A
Acrylics, 13
Amazon Annie (folk character), 34–35
Artist's watercolors, 13
Aspen, 6, 21, 32
Avocado, 6, 16, 32, 34, 36, 38
Awl, using a, 16, 18

B
Banjo Billy (musician), 110–113
Baseball pitcher, 52–57
Basswood, 6, 21
Big Ben (gunfighter), 92–93
Bowler, 58–59
Bucktooth Bill (western character), 86–87
Bucktooth Lil (western character), 88–89
Burrs, removing, 9
Businessman, 32–33

C
Cactus Jack (musician), 102–104
Calamity Jean (western character), 74–75
Cannonball Bates (sports character), 60–61
Carborundum abrasive dust, 9
Casey, the conductor (folk character), 46–47
Checkerboard, 12
Choirmaster, 107–109
Concertina players, 105–106
Concert pianist, 114–117
Conductor, 46–47
Coping saw, 70
Cottonwood, 6
Country singer, 102–103
Cowboys and cowgirls
   cowboy holding lariat, 76–77, 80–81
   cowboy rolling cigarette, 66–70
   cowboy with eye patch, 84–85
   cowboy with large nose, 78–79
   cowboy with prominent teeth, 86–87
   cowgirl with rifle, 74–75
   Mexican, 82–83
   three cowboys, 71–73
   woman with prominent teeth, 88–89

D
Danish oil, 13
Dorland's wax, 13
Dremel Moto-Tool, 4, 10, 11, 52
D-Vise, 100

F
Fancy Dan (folk character), 44–45
Farmer Fry (folk character), 38–39
Fast Draw (gunfighter), 94–95
Finishes, 13
Fireball Feeney (sports character), 52–57
Flash, the photographer (folk character), 40–43
Folk characters and caricatures
   businessman, 32–33
   conductor, 46–47
   couple (man and woman), 23–25
   farmer, 38–39
   German villagers, 18–20
   man holding flower, 44–45
   man "thinking," 30–31
   man wearing overalls, 28–29
   man whittling, 48–49
   man with beard, 36–37
   oriental character, 21–22
   Ozarks woman, 26–27
   photographer, 30–33
   woman with handbag, 34–35
   woman with shawl, 16–17
Football player, 62–63
Franny & Freddy (folk characters), 23–25
Fritz, Igor & Ivan (folk characters), 18–20

G
G. Cleff (musician), 107–109
Grid, 12
Gunfighters
   with guns drawn, 96–97
   with hands on holster, 92–95
   with shotgun, 98–100

H
Hands, carving, 10–11

J
Jed (folk character), 28–29
Jelutong, 6, 34
Jewellers' rouge, 9

K
Knives, 7–9
    patterns for, 8
    sharpening, 9

L
Lacquer, 13
Latex paint, 13
Linden, 6

M
Man holding flowers, 44–45
Man sitting on barrel, 30–31
Man wearing overalls, 28–29
Man with beard, 36–37
Maria (folk character), 16–17
Messrs. Sharps & Flats (musicians), 105–106
Mexican caricature, 82–83
Mr. Bucks (folk character), 32–33
Multipiece carving, 52–57
Musicians
    banjo player, 110–113
    choirmaster, 107–109
    concertina players, 105–106
    country singer, 102–104

N
Ned, the Thinker (folk character), 30–31
Noodle Nose Nelson (western character), 78–79

O
Oilstone, 9
Oriental character, 21–22
Ozarks woman, 26–27

P
Painting, 13
Paint thinner, 13
Patch (western character), 84–85
Patterns, enlarging or reducing, 12
Photographer, 40–41
Pianist and piano, 114–125
Pocketknives, 7
Poplar, 6
Professor Higginsniffer (musician), 114–125

Q
Quaking aspen, 6

S
Sandpaper, 13
Shotgun Sam (gunfighter), 98–100
Slim, Jim & Tim (western figures), 71–73

Slingin' Shufflebottom (sports figure), 62–63
Sports characters and caricatures
    baseball pitcher, 52–57
    bowler, 58–59
    football player, 62–63
    tennis player, 60–61
"Squaring-off," 12
Staining, 13
Strop, 9
Stubby (western character), 66–70
Sugar pine, 6
Sure Draw (gunfighter), 96–97

T
Taco Juan & Hamburger Harry (western characters), 82–83
Tennis player, 60–61
Tom, the Toquerville Kid (western character), 80–81
Tootsigoots, Belle of the Ozarks (folk character), 26–27
Trewax, 13
Turpentine, 13

U
Uncle Bub (western character), 76–77

V
Varnish, 13

W
Wan Qu Hung Hi (folk character), 21–22
Western heroes and heroines
    cowboy holding lariat, 76–77, 80–81
    cowboy rolling cigarette, 66–70
    cowboy with eye patch, 84–85
    cowboy with large nose, 78–79
    cowboy with prominent teeth, 86–87
    cowgirl with rifle, 74–75
    Mexican, 82–83
    three cowboys, 71–73
    woman with prominent teeth, 88–89
Whiskers Willie (folk character), 36–37
White pine, 6
Whittlin' Bill (folk character), 48–49
Whittling, as art, 4
Willow, 6
Wire edge, removing a, 9
Woman with handbag, 34–35
Woman with shawl, 16–17
Wood, 6
    soaking, 16
    using different types, 21, 32, 66
Wood scraps, 26, 34, 52, 74, 118